RUN THE MUSIC

Stories From A Creative Journey

ED TAR

Memoir

eta

ETA Publishing

California

Copyright by Ed Tar, 2024

ISBN: 978-1-7377699-2-7 Print
ISBN: 978-1-7377699-3-4 eBook
Library of Congress Control Number: 2024924663
Library of Congress
US Programs, Law and Literature Division
Cataloging in Publication Program
101 Independence Avenue, S.E.
Washington, DC 20540-4283

Events in this book are memories from the author's perspective
Book Design, Acapella Cover Design, Jennifer Givner.
Cover Background Art: Pat Gainor
Editor: Mike Robinson
All photos personal
Printed by Book Baby
First printing 2025

Publisher:
ETA, Inc
230 Venice Way
Venice, CA 90291

Also by Ed Tar

"REACHING FOR FIREFLIES"

To Pat, Heather and Donovan

"It isn't what we say or think that defines us, but what we do."

Jane Austin

MOVING ON

It was 1977. Inflation was high, as was unemployment, cost of living, and gas prices. "We Are the Champions," Queen's rock anthem, and Carly Simon's power ballad "Nobody Does It Better" stormed onto the music scene.

I was young, married, with a small daughter.

And I'd just quit my job.

My head was a fire hose of ideas and aspirations. Since meeting in college, my wife, Pat, and I had supported each other's dreams. We'd spend countless days talking about them and long nights at home going back and forth about what we wanted for our future. One reason I fell in love with her was how much we have in common.

When I told her of my plans to quit my job, she'd been busy shaping her acting career in Hollywood. I wanted to go it alone as an independent producer and was confident, with the small nest egg we'd built up, we could make this happen. We agreed not to touch any of Pat's income.

"We're going to have to tighten our belts for a while," I said to her anxiously, sitting at home after our daughter had gone to bed. "The vacation we planned has to be delayed, and we'll need to watch our spending on everything but essentials for a while."

On the surface, she didn't seem too fazed, but I knew her well enough to sense her concern. That's when I gently took her soft hand in mine, pulled her into my arms, and gave her a tender kiss. Holding her close, I said softly, "I'll make this work."

Her deep-green eyes looked into mine, and I saw the same excited gleam I'd seen the very first time we met. "Oh, good," she said, trying to sound confident, offering a smile as a kind of encouraging punctuation. She had always been the bright beam in our marriage. Her smile lifted my spirits and was just what I needed at this moment because tension filled my body. I was between excitement and fear.

A new chapter had begun in our journey.

***

For nearly two years, I'd been working in Los Angeles, running the office of a large Chicago media production company. My job was creating and producing large corporate films, TV commercials, and live stage shows. I was responsible for bringing in new clients and, after selling them on the company's services, producing their events from concept to completion.

When we decided to move to LA, a dream of ours for a long time, my father's old mocking words still haunted me: "Do you know what the hell you're doing, kid?"

I'd always been someone's employee and was growing frustrated. Working my "regular" job, I'd often run my hands through my hair and think, *Here I am again, an employee with other people setting the agenda, expecting me to dutifully follow along, performing what they want.*

I had my own dreams to achieve, and they weren't working for someone else.

Chicago management on several occasions directed who they wanted me to establish as a client. Once I succeeded in doing that, they'd take over, reaping the rewards for themselves, thus diluting my work to the point of soaking it, leaving it too heavy to lift.

Swirling in the back of my mind was the recurring thought *All my energy, ideas, and valuable time—day and night—are benefitting someone else, and management isn't sharing the wealth, so to speak.* There wasn't any single "ah-hah" moment or turning point that pushed me to say, *I want out of here!* It was more like a slow-moving trudge—through sludge. I was just a spoke in someone else's wheel and wanted to reap the rewards of working for myself.

Yet being an independent media producer, especially in highly competitive LA, would present a series of new challenges, obstacles, and questions:

How will my life change?

Can I support my family?

Will this journey provide the creative freedom and independence I long for?

Will I survive? At what price?

I was more than a little scared.

Over the previous several weeks, I often felt a light quiver in my stomach as I tossed and turned in bed at night, trying to erase doubts, to answer a million questions. Sometimes I was frozen with worry.

***

After moving to LA, Pat and I spent over a year in an apartment before purchasing a new home, a mere seven blocks from the sandy shore of the Pacific Ocean.

There were friends who questioned my timing of all this, of course. Despite my concerns, I felt optimistic about the prospects. For me, a journey's high point is achieving something independently or within the context of some worthwhile personal challenge.

There would be numerous hurdles to overcome, even from potential clients themselves. I envisioned a prospective client leaning back in his chair, arms folded over his girth, pupils narrowing, forehead furled, challenging me to provide a single good reason why he should hire me. If I wavered in my pitch, he was more than ready to say, "No." How would I react to that?

There were even more serious questions I needed to answer:

Will our savings be enough to support our lifestyle until my business produces some income?

Can I afford the business expenses necessary to set up an office?

Do I have what it takes to change and strike out on my own?

Can I be successful against much larger and stronger competition?

I found myself repeatedly scratching my skin, clearing my throat, and becoming easily irritated, especially at home with Pat and our daughter, Heather. At times, the dramatic journey I was embarking on felt at once overwhelming and exhilarating.

I'd be on my own more than at any point in my career, with no home office to call when things got tough. At the time, I didn't appreciate the importance of having a trusted support team: someone to talk with and bounce ideas off of; get feedback and advice from; and, when necessary, to offer a dissenting opinion.

Having engaged with large Fortune 500 clients, I knew they wanted an assurance that you weren't just a guy on the phone, calling from your bedroom. Understandable. Thus, one of my first orders of business—literally—was to open a small office. I remained undaunted. I was committing to the long haul.

And I needed an immediate cash outlay.

***

In any business, especially a new one, it's extremely important to keep overhead low. Many businesses go bust the first year when expenses spiral out of control. *Not going to happen to me,* I thought. *I'll hire a staff only when there is business to support one.*

For now, my focus was establishing an office and possibly getting a loan in case cash ran low. I had done this in Detroit three years earlier when I'd tried setting up my own business. The bank turned me down. Would it happen again?

I made an appointment at my bank. The loan officer sat in her small, glass-enclosed, ascetic-looking office, peering at me from behind a beige metal desk. Dressed conservatively in a white blouse and dark skirt, her hair stiffly sprayed, she maintained a pleasant manner as she nodded while listening to my story.

Handing me a sheet of paper, she said with a gleam in her eye, "We may be able to work something out. These are our current interest rates, which are very competitive."

I studied the list of rates for a moment but wasn't as cheerful as she was, thinking, *This is just another expense.* Turning to her, meeting that smile still pasted on her face, I said, "I need to think this through more carefully."

Her smile became a frown. "Our rates are very competitive, Mr. Tar."

"I'm sure they are."

Getting up, I thanked her, said goodbye, and never considered a bank loan again.

A much larger challenge, one I turned over in my mind time and time again, was where and how I would find new clients. There was a noncompete clause in my old company's contract that prevented me from soliciting any of their clients for one year after (voluntarily) leaving. This was a giant restriction and meant those client contacts I'd nurtured were worthless unless *they* initiated the call to me. So how was I going to start from scratch?

"If they paid you to secure a client," my attorney warned, "and now you're claiming it as yours, they can try to enforce the clause. Be careful. You don't want to get into some costly legal battle before even getting started."

He was right. But without new clients, my new journey was doomed to fail before even starting.

I closed my eyes and took in a calming breath. It wasn't going to be an easy journey. But then, if it were easy, anyone could do it.

Could I?

MEETING IRV

I wasn't going to make any money simply driving around LA *looking* for an office to rent. I needed to find one and decide. I'd driven past a small, single-story building several times, noticing the "Offices for Rent" sign out front. As it was just ten minutes from home, I told myself to check it out. Knocking on the office manager's door, I was greeted by a friendly, smiling gentleman.

"Hello," I said. "I noticed the for-rent sign. Are there any offices available?"

"Yes indeed. My name is Irv."

"Ed," I answered, returning his smile.

He extended his hand. "Nice meeting you, Ed. Please come in."

Irv was an older man, about sixty, with a slight build and graying hair. He leaned forward slightly when he walked and had a large belly that stressed the buttons of his light blue collared shirt.

"This is my wife, Sarah," Irv said, gesturing to a kind-looking woman seated at a desk and smiling broadly.

"Nice to meet you," she said.

Their office was large but spartan, containing only his and Sarah's desks, each with an Underwood manual typewriter, a phone, and small calculator. In one corner of the room sat a small table with a coffeepot, a few cups, and sugar. I could smell the aroma of recently brewed coffee. In the opposite corner stood a wooden coatrack holding a man's short jacket and a woman's sweater. A fading framed picture, a reproduction of a forest scene, adorned one wall, and a large calendar from an insurance company hung slightly askew on another. Music played low in the background from a small radio on the table.

"Please have a seat," Irv said, pointing to a chair in front of his somewhat disorganized desk. Pulling his chair closer to the desk, he slid a few papers aside, looked up, and asked, "How much space are you looking for?"

"Well . . . I need a small office. Maybe two."

"Hmn. We don't have any single offices, but we do have a beautiful three-office suite across the patio. It's a little over four hundred square feet."

"That's really more than I need right now," I said, slightly disappointed. "How much does it rent for?"

"Oh, I'm sure we can work something out. Would you like to see it?"

Accepting his nonanswer, I swallowed and said, "Why not? Never know."

He reached for the ring of keys on the wall behind his desk. "What do you need the office for? What business are you in?"

"I'm an independent producer," I said, "starting a new business. I work with corporate clients."

"I see. Uh-huh," he muttered, sneaking a quick glance at Sarah. "Let me show you the suite."

It felt as if he considered me a possible looky-loo, going through the motions of looking for an office.

***

We walked out across the patio to suite E. He unlocked the door, and as we went in, I was hit with a pervasive, musty smell, like an attic that hadn't been aired out in a while. The blinds were open halfway, and the hot summer sun cut through the window.

Irv left the door open and flipped the switch for the ceiling's fluorescent lights, which illuminated the plain beige walls and the slightly worn, marked-up carpet.

There were two offices, each large enough to hold a desk, a chair or two, and file cabinets. Both had a window. The third "office" was a small storage room the size of a couple closets. For the time being, I needed only one office for myself and one for an eventual assistant. The suite seemed a bit large, and I guessed the rent was going to be large as well.

"This space is nice," I said, trying not to sound committal or very interested, "but this third office seems more like a storage room."

"Call it what you want," Irv said, watching me eyeball the space, "but our last tenant used it as an office."

"Wow! Did they have a desk and chair in there?"

With a tinge of impatience in his voice, Irv answered, "I don't know. Maybe."

He reached over to wipe dust off a windowsill and swipe at a cobweb like a film of gossamer floating in the air.

"This suite also comes with parking in the rear," Irv added.

Standing in the center of the office, I nervously asked again, "What's the rent?"

He answered, "Three hundred sixty dollars a month on a yearly lease."

My muscles tightened. That was more than I had in mind, and I didn't want a year's lease just in case this place wasn't right for me.

"Is there any flexibility in the rent? I can't use that small space as an office."

He ignored my question. "Let me show you the parking area," Irv responded, sounding determined, "and then we'll go back to the office."

We stepped out, and he locked the door. We walked about fifty feet to the rear of the building and a paved, fenced parking area fit for about a dozen cars.

With the tone of a seasoned salesman, Irv said, "It comes with two parking spaces. There may be an open space you can use from time to time, and there's always street parking out front."

I scanned the parking area for a moment, feeling rushed. He'd turned and begun walking back to his office. I went to catch up.

As we reentered his office, Sarah looked up, grinning. "How'd you like it?"

The space is fine, I thought. *Now about that rent and lease terms.*

Trying to sound detached so they wouldn't think I was a slam dunk, I said, "It's larger than I need and over my budget."

Sarah replied, "Your business will grow, and you'll need some extra room."

Her positive attitude was encouraging but not enough for me to pull the trigger. Irv didn't say anything. He hung up the keys and sat down. I turned to him.

"The offices are nice, Irv," I said, "but is there any flexibility in the rent? That third office is pretty much useless to me."

He pondered, tapping his fingers on the desk. "Please have a seat." He glanced out the window toward the bright sunshine.

Once I sat, he turned back to me, stopped tapping, and leaned back in his chair.

"I'm sorry, that's what it rents for. What business are you in again?"

"I help companies launch new products."

"You're in advertising?"

"No. It's more marketing. I write and produce films and shows for large companies."

"And you're starting a new business?"

"Yes. I've always worked for somebody and decided to go out on my own."

He shifted in his chair. "I see. Uh ha. Well, the costs of maintaining the building never go down."

I sat silently, letting him have the floor, thinking, *That suite hasn't been rented in a while.*

His fingers began tapping again. "But as you're starting a business, maybe we can work something out. We might be able to lower the rent a bit, maybe 10 percent."

Still too high. Taking a deep breath, I exhaled and carefully countered, "How about 25 percent and a month-to-month lease?"

He looked down, shaking his head. "Can't do it. That's what we get for a small single office, not what we looked at."

I kept reminding myself, *Ed, keep it on the cheaper side.*

At first Sarah appeared not to have been listening, but then she stopped what she was doing and turned to Irv.

"Let me look in the file," she said, "and see if anyone in a smaller space might be leaving soon."

She got up, retrieved a folder from a filing cabinet, and took it to her desk, which, unlike Irv's, was very clean and organized. Quickly skimming through papers, she sighed and said, "It appears our tenants with any smaller space are going to be here for a while."

"What about the contractor in suite D?" Irv asked, a sharp tone in his voice. "He was talking about leaving. Is he?"

"I don't know," Sarah said, closing the folder. "That guy talks a lot but never decides. It doesn't look good for anything smaller. Sorry."

Feeling anxious but not ready to give up, I thought, *With the lagging economy, they probably don't get many inquiries. Advantage: me.*

I tried again. "Irv, if you'll let me have suite E for the price of the smaller suite, I'll take it right now." I recalled the old adage *A bird in the hand is worth two in the bush.*

"I can't do that!" he riposted, sounding exasperated. Sarah appeared startled and gave him a long stare.

A sneaking suspicion told me she might have wanted to talk with him alone, so I asked if I could walk through the space again. "It's not necessary for you to show me, Irv. I just want to get another feel for it."

He handed me the key ring. "Help yourself."

***

I crossed the patio to suite E, unlocked the door, and went in, leaving the door open for some fresh air. Looking around the offices, I tried imagining them with furnishings and people. Would they be comfortable for client meetings? Would I need some extra room as Sarah suggested?

Then I caught myself. *Wait a minute! Am I getting ahead of myself? The rent's too high and a one-year lease too long. Maybe I'm wasting my time. If I can't convince him to agree to my terms, it's time to move on.*

I returned to Irv's office. He and Sarah were talking and quickly stopped as I entered. Irv turned to me, sounding confident. "Anything different looking at it a second time?"

"It looks nice," I responded, handing him the keys, "but that tiny third office is of little use."

There was a change in his attitude. He took off his glasses. "Please, have a seat, Ed."

I sat.

"Sarah and I talked it over." He darted a glance at her. "And we can let you have suite E, and when the contractor moves out, you can move to the smaller suite."

He stopped, waiting for my reaction. I looked at Sarah. She offered a slight, satisfied smile.

Sucking in a deep breath, I asked, "Would I still have the option of staying in suite E at that time if I chose at the same rent?" I pulled my chair closer to his desk, quickly adding, "One day I may even need that large five-office suite at the front of the building. Right now, though, I only need a small space."

He turned slightly and rubbed the back of his neck. Small beads of perspiration glistened through his thinning hair.

"We can discuss that when and if it happens," he said with his voice rising. "Our expenses are going up. The utility bills are increasing. We just had a new roof installed. Taxes are high."

Sarah got up from her desk. "Would you like a cup of coffee, Mr. Tar?'

"No thanks."

Irv blurted out, "Maybe we can do something about the lease."

I wasn't sure what he meant and dared to ask, "Can I have a month-to-month lease?"

"We usually sign one-year leases."

I sensed a softening of his earlier statement that they "*only*" signed one-year leases. Trying to reassure them both, I told them I was married, had one child, and lived only a few miles away. I added, "My wife is an actress in TV and movies." Sometimes, especially in this town, people like to say they know so-and-so in the film or TV business.

Shifting to the edge of my seat, I reiterated that my clients were important corporations—neglecting, of course, to say I didn't have a single client. Yet.

Irv gave another quick glance at Sarah, who responded with a slight nod. He looked back at me and, with a tinge of reluctance in his voice, said, "Okay, since you're starting a business, we'll let you have it at your price. Just for six months, though, and we'll see where we are at that time."

Trying to contain my excitement, I offered a wide smile. "That'll be great! Thank you both very much." I stood up, shook Irv's hand, and stepped over to shake Sarah's. "I'll be moving in within the week."

As I left, my feet barely touched the ground. I hurried to my car parked on the street, got in, and screamed the "YES!" that I had swallowed in Irv's office.

Driver's window open and a fresh breeze caressing my face, I drove home to tell Pat the good news. She had been as anxious as me about the new journey I was embarking on—actually *we* were embarking on.

I rushed into the house, excited. "Honey!" I hollered. "Honey!"

"Yes. Be right there."

She came into the room when I broke out in a wide smile. "I did it! I have an office and am ready to go!"

She screamed. We hugged and stood there holding each other, swaying side to side.

Deep inside, a thought nagged me: *Did I make the right decision?*

"STAY IN TOUCH"

The week flew by. On a warm, sunny morning, a small truck with the words "New and Used Discount Office Furniture" painted on its side pulled up in front of the building to deliver my first investment: a used wooden desk, two slightly worn office chairs, and a gray metal file cabinet with a few scratches. I was anxious and excited— piece by piece, the dream was becoming a reality.

Irv must have seen the truck because as the two burly guys began unloading, he came out of his office.

"Morning!" he said. "Moving day?"

"Yes!" I answered energized, ready to charge ahead.

"If you're interested, I have a desk in our storage room out back. It's in good shape. Be happy to sell it. Want to see it?"

"Sure. What're you asking for it?"

"Oh, we can work something out. How 'bout a hundred dollars?"

"Will you take fifty?"

He sighed. "You're getting a steal, but okay, fifty dollars."

***

When all was settled, I didn't have time to sit around and admire a couple of used desks in mostly unfurnished and unoccupied offices. I was anxious to have it all come alive with busy people and ringing phones. It was time to generate some income.

Soon the telephone became my closest friend. I knew many creative people in Hollywood—writers, directors, designers, camera operators—and it was important to keep those relationships fresh. Everyone was friendly and encouraging. "Good luck." "Hope it works out." "Call if you need anything." The fact is they were looking for jobs themselves. These were the people I'd need when I had a film or show to produce. They couldn't help me find clients. I appreciated their being there, but I was on my own when it came to digging up business.

The periodic brief conversations with them helped me keep my sanity. One in particular hit home. Julian, a friend in San Francisco, told me, "Ed, I set up my business two years ago, and it's been the toughest two years of my life. I'm now seeing business pick up and believe I made the right call. Hang in there, buddy. You can do it!"

Meanwhile I called every phone number on my list of potential clients.

Some of the people at the companies I called took my calls; others didn't. Those who did patiently listened to my story about my new business and said, "Stay in touch."

That was it. Sitting alone with a cup of black coffee on my desk, I placed call after call as soon as I arrived each morning. My calendar looked like a call center, only I was making the calls, not receiving them.

Many thoughts and doubts crossed my mind. Was my timing right in going out on my own? The economy was not in good shape and wasn't getting any better. Corporate clients were becoming tighter with spending. What had I done?

Although I had considered many questions before venturing out on my own, it was a lot different when reality was staring me in the face. The challenges were there and touchable. They were not new to me. I reflected on other challenges growing up in a large, somewhat dysfunctional family in Detroit, how even in the dead of winter, when there was no heat in the house, little food, and arguing parents, I managed to garner the drive to keep moving forward and get a job on my own at the age of nine, save up enough money to buy a guitar and pay for my own music lessons at eleven, and buy a car at age sixteen, paying for it entirely myself with cash I'd saved. But that was then. This was now—I had my own family to care for and bills to pay.

Weeks turned well into months. I fought my doubts and kept fighting for that first sale. It's been said, "Most sales happen after the sixth call. Most people stop calling after the third." There may be some truth in that.

One problem: I didn't consider myself a real salesman. Salesmen were those who usually wore a suit, shiny shoes, and white shirts too tight around the neck, who never lacked for something to say. They knew how to smooth talk, how to wine and dine a client, tell a good—often exaggerated—story, and they never missed a beat getting the order. In my situation, I felt there was only one thing to do—be my own version of that kind of guy—and I was struggling.

Then something happened.

***

Before leaving my last job, I'd had a brief contact with a gentleman named Ron, head of merchandising at a large carpet manufacturer in City of Industry, California. It was unusual to see carpet manufacturers in California since the epicenter of the carpet world was Dalton, Georgia. At the time, Dalton was to the carpet industry what Detroit had been to the auto industry in the fifties.

I knew nothing about carpets, and frankly, it sounded like a dull business. My only exposure to carpets was when Pat dragged me into a carpet store, and we stood there as some guy with an accent slowly rolled back pieces of carpet lying on a large table in the center of the room, telling us he would give us a great deal.

 But now was not the time to be picky.

After weeks of coming up empty with others, I reached out to Ron at the carpet manufacturer and was surprised he took my call. He seemed genuinely interested in what I was doing. During our brief conversation, I asked if he had any time to meet to tell him more.

I sat there clutching the phone to my ear, fingers crossed on my other hand, praying not to hear another noncommittal "Stay in touch."

"When would you like to get together?" he asked.

Unsure I'd heard him correctly, I cleared my throat and stumbled in my response: "How does next week sound?"

Holding my breath, the three seconds he took to respond felt like ten.

"Thursday next week is good for me," he said. "How 'bout you?'

"Sure, 10 a.m.?"

"Okay," he said. "See you then."

Shivering with excitement, I hung up the phone, stood up, threw a punch into the wind, and screamed another "Yes!"

I looked around the empty office, took a glance out the window at the bright sunshine, and thought, *This might just work out.* My persistence and calls over the past weeks had landed me my first meeting with a potential client. I called Pat to tell her the good news.

Before our meeting, I read everything to do with the carpet industry. My heart beat fast as I drove to their offices, trying to anticipate questions he might ask and rehearsing my answers out loud as I sped along the freeway.

Arriving, I almost felt I was in a carpet store. Carpet samples surrounded me and filled the tables in the lobby. The receptionist told me Ron was expecting me and directed me to his office.

His door was open and he was seated, working at his desk. I gave a slight nervous knock.

He glanced up. "Ed?" he said. "Come on in."

He came around the desk. We shook hands. "How are you?" he asked.

"I'm fine," I said. "It's nice to meet you, and thank you for taking time to see me."

Ron was in his late forties, had a big smile, stood just shy of six feet, and sported dark, thinning hair. Wearing a white shirt and tie, he appeared very businesslike. No suit jacket.

His office was rather small, appearing even smaller with carpet sample boards, each about a foot square, on the floor and walls.

"Please have a seat," he said, gesturing to the chair in front of his desk. "Excuse the mess. These are some sample boards of our new line we'll be introducing at our upcoming show."

He asked some of the questions I had anticipated about the films and shows I'd produced and my key creative team. I answered and listened intently as he told me they were planning their first ever national show in Newport Beach, California, for their dealers and managers from across North America. These were the people responsible for moving the carpets to and through the retail stores. He was interviewing a few producers in Southern California to produce the show for him. I asked who, but he didn't want to say.

With passion in his voice, he said, "We want this event to be fun and exciting to get our message out. How would you handle a show with original music, a cast of performers, film segments, several live presentations from multiple stage positions around the room, and an exciting range of new products?"

I took a deep breath and replied slowly, "*Verrry* carefully."

A relaxed smile crossed his face before he laughed, releasing some of the tension I was feeling and surely he was too. It lightened up our meeting.

Previously, Ron had worked back east for a company that was very active in introducing new products with large entertaining shows. He told me he knew what it took to produce a live show.

Clearing my throat, I assured him I did too—although, now working on my own, it would be a challenging new venture. I couldn't simply pick up the phone for free advice from a staff in Chicago. My instincts and my gut would play a bigger role in my decisions.

It had been a few months since I'd sat in front of a prospective client. Could he see my nervousness? How close was he to pulling back?

Ron tilted his head back and raised his arm to look at his watch. "They'll be going on their midmorning break in the factory soon. Would you like to see how carpets are made?"

I didn't care, but this was a potential client.

"Do you have time?" he pressed.

"Sure," I said, adding, "I've been through many plants from aerospace to automobiles to motorcycles and even breweries, but never a carpet mill."

"Well, good," he said, getting up. "Now you'll see how we do it."

We walked down two halls into the factory.

"This is where it all happens," he said, projecting his voice above the noise of the machines moving long strands of yarn from giant beams, like spools of thread, through automated looping devices capable of making carpet in a rainbow of every imaginable color, pattern, and texture. The entire production was impressive.

Twenty minutes later, we were back in his office. He sat down, quickly checked a couple written messages that had been set on his desk while we were gone, and pushed them aside. I sensed he was running out of time.

Up to that point, he'd told me a great deal of what he had coming up, and I'd told him everything about me, but he hadn't invited me to submit a proposal for his event.

My mind raced. *I have to bring it up. Why else would he spend this much time with me unless he was interested in what I could bring to his party?*

With rising nerves, I said, "Ron, I'd welcome an opportunity to prepare a creative proposal for your show."

Leaning forward, placing his hands on top of his desk, he smiled. "Yes, of course. As noted, we are also considering two other producers."

"I understand." Keeping my demeaner calm, I went on, "I would personally be involved in every aspect of your show, from the initial creative approach to the actual staging and execution."

He reached for some papers on the credenza behind his desk and handed them to me. "We've written our objectives and information about the product lines we'll be introducing. This might help you understand what we're looking to achieve."

I took a quick look and asked if I could take them with me.

"By all means," he said.

They'd scheduled a look at all three producer proposals in a single day. The only time left for me was late afternoon, when people start losing steam. In my current situation looking for work, I would have been happy to present my proposal at 3 a.m. if needed. Grateful, I thanked him for the opportunity.

He walked me to the lobby. We shook hands, and I left.

***

I get excited taking an idea and making it a reality for all to see and experience. It's satisfying and rewarding to know I took on a challenge and succeeded.

The theme they selected for the show was "The California Look," and my job was to demonstrate how I would tie it into their show. That wouldn't be easy.

I spent the entire next three weeks preparing the lengthy twenty-page proposal, including the names and backgrounds of the creative team I had assembled, all Hollywood music and stage professionals. Along with the team, I invested in preparing beautiful color stage renderings, samples of music possibilities, graphics, and film samples. Seeing the entire show and all the elements come together made me happy.

Had it been worth it? I was about to find out.

I arrived early to set up for my presentation. The conference room's twelve-foot-long table, with ashtrays, water glasses, and two pitchers of water, would easily seat the group of five, allowing me room to maneuver with stage renderings and a visual demonstration.

The room was windowless, with plain, nondescript beige walls on which were hung a couple advertising photos of happy children playing on carpet. Another featured a woman's hand sinking into plush carpet. *Coronado: Plush and comfortable*, read the ad copy across the bottom.

The company executives casually strolled in, a couple carrying notepads. My nerves tingled with tense energy. I said hello, and we exchanged greetings.

Ron stood up, cleared his throat, and outlined why we were there, though they knew. He introduced me, gave a brief background about what I did, and let me have the floor. He had told me earlier that Don, the vice president and general manager, might be taciturn.

Soon after I began, Don had a question.

He wasn't taciturn at all.

Stretching his neck up and reaching to slightly pull the knot in his tie, he asked, "Who are you working with now?"

"Well, I'm—"

"Who are your clients?" he cut in.

That was tricky. I made steady eye contact with him.

"Since starting my own business," I said, nervousness in my voice, "you would be my first client and receive 100 percent of my attention."

After Don's question, no one else said anything.

I was shakier than I'd like to admit but confident my experience would assure them I understood what they expected to achieve with their upcoming event. My mouth was dry. Taking a drink of water, I cleared my throat and laid out the show in detail.

As suspected, it being late afternoon, their energy level was waning. They shifted in their chairs, having just sat through two earlier presentations.

When finished, I passed out a written copy of my presentation. A couple of them thumbed through the pages but sat quietly. They liked my ideas but were concerned about executing them without a large staff of full-time employes. The two other companies that had presented earlier that day had apparently emphasized their size and depth of staff. That was my weak point—but also my strongest.

"I'll bring only the best people to work on your show," I told them, "and won't be saddled with having to use a staff person just because they're on staff, even if they're not the most ideal or qualified."

One of them quickly commented, "We want the best people."

I worried they didn't have many questions. Did that mean they weren't interested, that they'd already made up their minds, or was it just my being overly nervous and sensitive?

Ron stood up to wind down the meeting. "Thank you, Ed. Interesting ideas. I'll be in touch if we need any further information, and please feel free to give me a call if you have any questions."

I thanked him and the others. Ron walked me to the lobby. I said goodbye and hurried to my car.

As I drove back to my office, the speedometer hit eighty-five in a sixty zone. My mind was racing as fast. It was a while before I noticed and thought to slow down.

THE FIRST SHOW

With the meeting filling my mind, I was unable to sleep well that night. I woke early the next morning and rushed to my office. I needed an answer—I had a family counting on me.

"Keep knocking on those doors," my mother told me once when I was eight years old. She had me going door-to-door on the street where we lived in Detroit, trying to sell her crocheted doilies. Once, I sold three pieces and proudly showed her.

"Good," she said. "Now go on the other side of the street, knock on those doors, and see if you can sell some more."

***

As I was waiting to hear their decision about my proposal to them, days passed, and I kept knocking on other doors and made contact with an RV manufacturer headquartered in Riverside, California.

Not only were they one of the largest producers of RVs in North America, with manufacturing facilities stretching across the US and Canada, they had several hundred dealers. With that many dealers, they were similar to auto companies who held annual new vehicle announcement shows and sent out a barrage of product films to their dealers. *If car companies do it*, I thought, *what about RVs?* I had never even been in an RV before, but I resolved to find out about them.

This was a terrific opportunity—a niche to exploit. I called them and was directed to a training manager, who agreed to hear more about what I had to offer.

We set up a meeting for the following week. I didn't have much interest in making training films but took the opportunity to meet him and use it as a first step in with the company. He didn't have any budget and gave me the names of the people in marketing who handled media and their shows.

***

Coming back from Riverside at an aching, traffic-slowed ten miles an hour, I glanced at the drivers in the cars next to me and wondered, *Does that person make this drive back and forth to work every day? It could add up to four hours a day in the car. What a waste of time.*

I patted myself on the back, happy to have set up my business so as to avoid a daily freeway commute.

The sun was ebbing when I arrived back at my office. I set my briefcase down and saw a message from Ron. It was too late to call him back.

Since my presentation, he and I had talked by phone once to answer a couple lingering questions. Was this more questions, or had they reached a decision? Were they choosing me?

A nervous, empty feeling deepened in my stomach as I left the office and drove home.

***

Feeling fidgety over dinner with Pat and Heather, I mentioned the call.

"It was too late to return his call today," I said to Pat. "You know I would have otherwise." I couldn't get the phone call out of my head. "What if he was calling to say, 'Sorry, we chose someone else'?"

"Relax," she said, smiling. She reached over and gave me a one-handed shoulder massage. "He's probably going to give you the job."

"Let's hope so." After a lull, I repeated anxiously, "The message was just to call him. It was too late to do it."

"Let's forget it for tonight and have dinner," she said, passing me the potatoes. "Heather, honey, take some vegetables. Remember, you still have homework to do."

"I know," she said, sounding like she didn't need to be reminded and not interested in our conversation.

Heather, being our only child, enjoyed our full attention. Even though she was nine years old, her energy and determination to achieve what she set her mind to were unstoppable. Her school report cards consistently carried mostly As, and she enjoyed a long list of friends.

That night, as I lay in bed, my mind raced back to my presentation. *What more could I have done?* Pat was silent, but I'm sure, in my tossing and turning, I kept her awake, too.

***

The next morning, rushing through a shower and shave, I skipped breakfast and hurried to my office.

As I sat alone, my mind sped through all the possible scenarios of what he might say: "You got the job." "We chose someone else." "We haven't reached a decision yet." "We need more information."

I took a deep breath, made the sign of the cross, picked up the phone—then immediately set it down. I got up and walked around the office, trying to settle my nerves. My throat was dry. I took a sip of coffee and dialed his number on the black rotary phone.

"Hello. This is Ron," he answered.

"Hi, Ron. Ed Tar, returning your call."

"Ed, glad you called. How are you doing?"

I thought, *What have you decided?*

"Fine," I replied, trying to sound calm.

"We've gone through the proposals," Ron said calmly, "and wanted to let you know we made a decision."

I froze. My breathing stopped. My hand tightened on the phone. It was only a beat or two before he said:

"We would like you to produce the show for us."

I choked up. There was a lump in my throat, and I barely got the words out of my mouth.

"That's great, Ron! Thank you very much. That makes me very, very happy. You won't be disappointed."

"I know we won't," he said with an audible smile. "You were tuned into our needs more than the other producers who presented, and your creative ideas sealed the deal.

Everyone in the meeting felt the same way. I'd like to get started soon. How about the first of next week?"

"Just tell me when," I said gleefully.

We spent a minute agreeing to a time. I thanked him again, then hung up the phone, took a deep breath, looked up, and, eyes watering, mouthed the words *Thank you*.

I was ecstatic. My first job as an independent producer. I wasn't king of the world but felt like the king of my own future. I called Pat to tell her the good news.

"I knew you would get it!" she cried. "I just knew it! Wonderful!"

That evening when I arrived home, Pat and Heather had "Congratulations" balloons hung up for me. That made me feel special. As we exchanged hugs, I felt for the first time I'd made the right move, and things at work might be okay.

***

The goal: a powerful, highly energetic, and memorable show to launch their newest products to important retailers and dealers across the US. The budget was tight. Could I pull this off? Would it be any good? I'd triumphed in getting the job. Now I needed to *do* the job.

For the next two months, I spent 90 percent of my time working on this show, putting my key creative team together. Tom, a creative Chicago writer I'd used once before, wrote the live sketches in the show. Don, a very talented Hollywood composer, wrote the music. He had been the musical director for Ice Capades, and we had collaborated before. I chose Alex, a sharp-tongued New York choreographer, to skillfully handle the direction and cast. Others on the team were creative people I'd previously worked with in Hollywood. To shoot some of the film segments, I called on Mike, who found time between his motion picture stints to help me out. Anita coordinated development of the speaker visual support.

As the date of the show drew closer, my days grew longer—thirteen, fourteen hours became the norm. Sleep dropped to five hours a night from seven, and my irritability level increased dramatically, especially at home. Pat didn't appreciate that on a couple nights a week, I'd sit at the Bob's Big Boy near home and indulge my vice for hot fudge sundaes and coffee. Better than a bar, right? I was being unfair.

Some nights I was off to the hockey rink for a game of pickup hockey. It was important to clear my mind and relieve the stress after a busy day. Hockey always did that. My younger brother, Les, and I had played together back in Detroit. Now that we both lived in California, we continued. Les was single, a free spirit, and a very good player. Our conversations and stories we shared riding back and forth to the rink tightened the bond we had.

***

A week before the show, cast rehearsals began in Hollywood. The four energetic cast members, two women and two men, in their mid-twenties, were full of smiles. They were quick to learn their lines, and Alex did a wonderful job during rehearsals with the dance routines. No one acted like a prima donna, and they got along well.

While rehearsals continued, anticipation increased as we began setting the stage at the hotel; hanging lights, sound, drapes, screens, and projectors; and preparing for the final onstage dress rehearsals.

It's unusual when strong-willed, creative people who don't know each other are thrown together without some major conflict or problem needing to be resolved. Happily, there was none on this show. My creative team—the performers, the technicians, and the stagehands—all had a common goal: to produce a successful show.

On show day, I walked to the control booth, a routine I did on every show I produced, to tell them "run the music," signaling the doors were about to open.

A few minutes later, the hall was filled, the audience settled, and the lights went down. Our energetic cast burst onto the stage. They kept the action and excitement moving with short vignettes and specially written musical numbers singing the praises of each new product. The excitement continued on two smaller satellite stages in the room where the products were revealed.

The hour-long event came together as planned. The managers, carpet dealers, and retailers in the audience enthusiastically responded with applause and cheers. If it was possible to make carpet exciting, we did it! Backstage, I saw Ron bursting with enthusiasm.

"That was perfect," he said, giving a dramatic fist pump.

My confidence shot up, and my passion for producing intensified as I searched for the next show.

***

A few months later, Ron asked me to produce a smaller event at the exclusive Surf and Sand Resort in Laguna Beach, California, for their parent company. He said we wouldn't use performers in this one, just visual support and short filmed segments supporting executive presentations.

During an afternoon break, while the ballroom was being converted for the evening award ceremonies, I decided to get out of the hotel for a relaxing walk on the beach.

It was a cool, dreary, overcast day. The beach was deserted. I slipped off my shoes in the soft sand and walked alone. The chill of the ocean breeze was refreshing. I stepped around pockets of seaweed and small pieces of deadwood.

Venturing farther down the beach, I began feeling uneasy, my body turning red with itchy welts and bumps. Had I touched something in the sand, or had I been stung? This had never happened before. I cut the walk short to return to the hotel to wash off whatever was causing this.

Back at the hotel, the discomfort increased. I entered the lobby, ignoring the smiley front desk clerk's "Good afternoon, sir," and rushed toward the elevator. Somewhat panicked, I entered my room and looked in the mirror—I was as red as Santa Claus. Hurrying into the shower, I grabbed a bar of soap, turned on the hot water, and began scrubbing the welts. The hot water made it more uncomfortable.

My entire body was strawberry red and hot. Lightheaded and weak, I carefully stepped out of the shower and turned up the room air conditioner, hoping the cool air would offer some relief. My room faced the ocean. I opened the window for the breeze.

I lay on the bed, trying to understand what was going on. My body tingled. *Will this go away?* I certainly couldn't go down to the ballroom looking and feeling like this. *What should I do?*

With the rhythmic sound of the surf rolling below, I fell into a deep sleep, waking almost an hour later. The itchy redness was subsiding. Some marks persisted.

I slowly got up, shivering. My skin was sensitive. I closed the window, turned down the air, got dressed, and went to the ballroom, where rehearsals for the evening awards were about to begin.

Still shaken and wondering if I looked any different, I mentioned to my stage manager what had happened. He didn't offer any answers, but it made me feel better just telling someone.

***

Although the carpet shows were successful, and they paid me quickly without any hassle, their next show was nearly a year away with no guarantee they'd select me to produce it. That wasn't going to work. I needed another client badly. Pat's work was uneven at the time, and our bills kept coming in. There was growing dissension at home.

"All you talk about is work when you get home," Pat said, "and you don't get here some nights until Heather is already in bed. She wants to see her father and tell you what she's doing at school."

A feeling of guilt filled my body, and it wasn't the first time.

"I'll make it a point to get home earlier and spend time with her and you," I said.

Pat looked at me with doubt in her eyes. "I know you're busy, but I've heard that before."

I reached out for her hand. "This time it'll be different. Promise."

Rejecting my gesture, her chin rising, she said, "We'll see."

Pulling myself away from work with a thousand things on my mind was a struggle in those early days.

The next morning, my attention turned back to the RV company, with whom I'd stayed in contact over the past couple months. I had time now to intensify my calls and was able to set up a meeting with both the vice president and the marketing director.

Arriving for that first meeting, I was on edge and engaged in some self-talk: *You can do this, Ed. Look at how well those carpet shows went.*

We met in the first-floor office of Earl, the division vice president. It was modest in size, with a credenza behind the desk containing two photos of his family, a small potted plant, and a short stack of papers. The office was more conservative than one might expect from someone under constant pressure, running an entire division of a publicly traded company on the NYSE.

I took my seat in one of the two chairs in front of his desk. Sitting in the other was the marketing manager, Harry.

In his early forties, Earl was focused. His steely dark eyes didn't wander, and he didn't waste words or raise his voice. Dressed neatly in slacks and an embossed shirt with the company logo, he sat up straight. His hair was neatly combed.

Harry, the marketing manager, was more animated and expressive. He spoke rapidly, smiled easily, and often used hand gestures when talking, unlike Earl, who was more subdued.

In my calls leading up to this meeting, they told me they were planning a first-ever national dealer show and seeking someone to produce it for them. It might have surprised them that I wasn't the typical sales guy who made boastful statements and promises.

"You told us your business is new," Earl said, peering into my eyes. His voice was measured but friendly. "Tell us how you'd handle a large show like what we have in mind."

"Okay," I answered, shifting in my chair, uncrossing my legs. I hoped he couldn't hear the nervousness in my response.

He continued, "Would this be the first show since starting your company?"

Hearing the phrase "starting your company" sounded awkward. In my mind, "company" meant a big operation with hundreds of people. That was the last thing I wanted.

I steadied myself, my heart pounding.

"I just completed two shows for a major carpet company, so I'm free to devote full time to yours."

"When were those shows?" he quickly asked. "Where? How large were they? What did you do?"

I answered while Harry was busy jotting notes. He looked up. "Do you have a staff?

"Counting a wide cadre of contracted freelance people," I said, trying to sound reassuring, "my staff is limitless. It's more efficient and beneficial for you this way too."

His eyes shifted to Earl, who quickly asked, "How so?"

"If I had a large staff, my first obligation, naturally, would be to keep them busy, as any business would, even if they were not proficient in what you needed."

I waited for a reaction. There was none.

"My way of operating," I continued, "is to collaborate with you to identify your unique needs and objectives and to create a show that fulfills them.

Harry gave a darting glance at Earl. His body rigid, he turned to me, nervously flipping a pencil back and forth in his hand and asked,

"You use only freelance people?"

"I build a team specifically experienced in what is required to achieve *your* goals," I responded quickly. "Each person on the team is contracted to perform a specific task."

I could feel small beads of perspiration on my forehead. My mouth was dry. The large size of the show they had in mind was a bit overwhelming. At the time, I was still a one-man band, so to speak, full of ideas and a deep determination to succeed.

They were liberal with the details about what they wanted, and our meeting went longer than expected. *That is a good sign*, I told myself.

Being careful not to promise something that couldn't be delivered, I leaned forward in my chair.

"You'll have my 100 percent attention if I'm given the opportunity to work with you. There's no other project at this time to divert it."

Earl sat back. His eyes remained trained on me.

"I'd welcome the opportunity to return with some ideas and a creative proposal."

His head went back slightly. "Just so we're clear: we don't pay for proposals."

"Understood."

My thoughts raced. *Come on, give me a break, just this one time.*

"Super," he said, looking at me, then at Harry. "We're open to seeing what you think we should do with this meeting."

Excited, I smiled broadly.

"That's great. Thank you."

Once they knew I wouldn't charge for a proposal, Harry sank back in his seat, seemingly relieved. We spent the last half hour discussing details about this first-time event. I was taking notes as quickly as possible. It was coming at me fast. I could do this.

GROWING

There was no time to waste. I had to get a creative proposal together and reached out to a friend I'd worked with before.

A veteran Detroit writer, Bob would be a natural fit to work with me. He was fast, understood the corporate mind, and knew how to write and present a dynamic proposal. Bob was a showman. His background as an amateur magician helped his timing. He knew how to tell a story and demanded attention. He was six feet tall and a bit overweight, had dark thinning hair, and smoked a pipe, which added to his wise, knowing persona.

I flew him to LA for our presentation. If we were awarded the show, he'd write it.

Richard, who had created the stage renderings for me on the carpet show, would do the same for this one. Presenting large colored renderings was an effective way to give the client a visual look at the planned stage setting. Such a sneak peek was important in this case, being their first experience with an event this large.

Two weeks later, Bob and I made a compelling pitch in their boardroom to the division VP and marketing manager as well as the company president. Their demeanor was friendly, but I detected seeds of anxiety. They interrupted with numerous questions. They made many notes, nodding as we went on, adding mostly monosyllabic commentary such as "Okay," or "I see," or, more encouragingly, "Super."

Bob did an outstanding job with the proposal. I reinforced it when needed, answered questions, provided cost information, and assured them the ideas we were presenting would be successful. Bob and I were a good team.

We didn't recommend anything complicated. This was their first national dealer meeting. They wanted a straight live stage presentation with highlights about their products, backed up with visual and film support, plus a live exciting product reveal using special effects, lights, and sound. Nope. Not complicated.

***

After our presentation, I didn't have the luxury of sitting around for what might be weeks before they reached a decision. I had to keep pursuing potential clients. A Japanese auto company was on my radar, as was the successful newspaper in Long Beach. It was difficult to make contact with the right people at both places as they were often unavailable.

I'd spent a great deal of time and money pitching the RV show, and my mind wasn't fully focused on calling other potential clients just yet. Naively, I expected clients to make fast decisions—a "you in or out?" kind of thing. In the corporate world, with its layers of people and politics, decisions were not made quickly.

Bob offered to fly back to meet them again if needed. I said no, having devoted enough time and money at this point. Replaying in my mind what we presented, I considered everything to be on target and the budget reasonable. What more could we have done?

As we entered the third week without a decision, my impatience grew, and I decided to call them. Harry took my call.

"Call me next Monday," he said.

Anxious, I asked, "Do you need anything else from me?"

His voice was calm, almost dismissive. "No. We have everything we need."

If they have everything they need, I thought, *what's holding up a decision? Did they decide to use someone else?*

I hung up. *Is this all worth it?* I asked myself that question often those first years.

It was incredibly stressful and nerve-racking lining up clients, making presentations, producing an event, then worrying about it and the next one. It was a never-ending cycle, but I had no choice. The decision to forge my own path had been mine and mine alone. What else could I do? Where else could I go? I wasn't about to be anyone's employee again.

Patience is important, but too much of it and I might be out of business as fast as I got in.

Arriving in my office early the following Monday, I sat there apprehensively, had two cups of black coffee, and was ready to call Harry. My leg shook as I sucked in some deep breaths and dialed his number.

He answered, sounding upbeat, and didn't hesitate. "I'm glad you called early as my day is filling up with meetings."

My stomach fluttered and my heart pounded. Maybe he could hear the tension in my voice when I said, "You said to call you today. Is this a good time?"

"Yes, it's perfect." He let out a small chuckle. "You probably want to know our decision, and I don't blame you. I would too if I were in in your shoes. After reviewing all the proposals, we liked your ideas, and if you're available, we would like to work with you."

My mind was racing, as were my words, from the coffee. *If I'm available?* I don't think I took a breath before answering.

"Yes, of course," I said. "Terrific! It's going to be fun working with you, and the meeting is going to be great!"

"We think it will be too," he said.

Three days later, I drove out to see him and begin the work of producing their first national dealer show. There were two shows, one in Los Angeles for the West Coast dealers and one in Louisville for dealers from the East Coast and Canada.

They couldn't have been more pleased with the scripts Bob wrote. The creative visual support, staging, lighting, sound, and direction all came together, but not without some tension-filled moments at the convention center in Louisville. It was a union house, and nothing was done there without using union people.

Tony, one of my backstage projectionists whom I'd worked with before, was a union steward in Nebraska and carried a yellow card, allowing him to work in other union venues. He knew union language and was able to smooth out concerns of the local union about some of our crew not having a yellow card. In some places they wouldn't be allowed to work without it.

I saw him in an animated conversation backstage with the local steward and stayed away. Once the steward left, Tony told me, "He'll allow our guys to work without adding more labor." I was relieved as that saved me a lot of money.

The meeting, from the client's and dealer's enthusiastic responses, was a success. I was grateful and hoped it set me up for further work with them.

It felt good knowing I'd beaten out one particular production company that had bid against me, whose management, I was told, showed up for their presentation wearing T-shirts with "*Hollywood*" splashed across the front. That's not the way to look when approaching a corporate client with a bunch of money—and their reputation—on the line.

I was relieved, having snagged two important clients in such a short time. This was a turning point and kicked my business forward. It bolstered my confidence when transitioning from one client to another across different industries without missing a beat and without a large, expensive staff. I often repeated to myself, *Keep your overhead and expenses to a minimum if you want to succeed.*

Equally important was the fact that I'd won them over not as a staff member of some large media company with vast resources but on my own. I'd proven myself, and my business, capable of handling an entire production from concept to execution. "Take *that*, you doubters!"— doubters such as the large soft drink company's senior sales VP who told me, "I can't see how you could produce our bottler meeting and do it all being so small."

My carpet client was a questionable future prospect. They were planning to move their operations to Georgia. Maintaining a long-distance client would be costly and difficult for someone of my current size.

Around this time, I hit a major milestone and hired my first full-time employee, an assistant named Laura. She had been working for me freelance since day one. Laura was smart, reliable, and organized, and she had strong social skills, making for a good first impression on the phone with clients. She handled anything and everything I asked of her.

***

During my second year as an independent producer, things were about to change and to become more demanding, especially at home.

One day, I walked into the house, and Pat greeted me with a bright smile. She always had a smile for me, but today it seemed bigger.

"Hi, honey," she said. "How was your day?"

"Fine," I responded with a hug and a kiss.

Standing close, holding my hand, she said, "I went to the doctor today."

"What's going on?" I replied, gently breaking away and walking to the front closet to hang my jacket. I closed the door and turned around. She stood there, still smiling broadly, her eyes gleaming.

"Guess what?" She paused a second with her eyes wide. "I'm pregnant."

I stuttered, "What? Are you sure?"

"Yes! The baby is due in May."

"May! Incredible!" I looked into her sparkling eyes and wrapped her in my arms. My mind raced. My heart was pounding. "Tell me about it. What'd the doctor say? Are you okay? Would you like to sit down?" I reached for her arm to guide her to the sofa. "Where would you like to sit?"

"I'm fine," she said with a slight chuckle. "I haven't told Heather yet she's going to be a big sister."

Anxiety began bubbling under my excitement.

How would we handle a growing family, my new business, and Pat's career?

Building a solid career in Hollywood takes dedication, time, and being able to accept rejection. Pat went to every audition with high hopes and many times returned home with her hopes dashed, not being selected for the part. She fought the negative, always looking on the bright side.

Since moving to California three years earlier, her Hollywood career had progressed. She'd appeared multiple times on the popular long-running daytime soap *Days of Our Lives* and on several nighttime series, including Irwin Allen's made-for-TV movie *Flood*. I was in total support of her working, though worried at times about how she could handle it all.

She even enrolled in the Harvey Lembeck Comedy Workshop in Hollywood. Inspired by the talent there, including Robin Williams, she developed her own comedy routine and performed at the famous Comedy Store on Sunset Boulevard. I was proud sitting in the back watching her routine, and never knew she could do comedy as well as she did.

As we drove home together, she said, sounding concerned, "I was more nervous tonight than ever knowing you were there. My timing was off."

"You were great," I told her, "and so was your timing. The audience loved you. So do I."

Auditions would surely dry up when her pregnancy began to show. No one was hiring pregnant actors.

Years earlier when Pat was pregnant with our daughter, Heather, in Michigan, she was able to continue hosting her daily TV talk show, but now in Hollywood, she had to put her career on hold.

She always made every effort to be home when Heather arrived from school. Maybe it was because of our Midwest roots, but we were determined not to be absentee parents. We were both raised Catholic, and Pat's Irish family background was anything but "Hollywood." Her mother encouraged her to accomplish all she could with her career, while her father, although supportive of her career dreams, would have been happy if she had chosen a different path.

Pat and her father had always been very close. "I think I gained my curiosity from him," she said. "If I asked him a question or didn't understand a word, he'd stop what he was doing, and we'd look up the answer together."

It was his creative eye in painting giant, colorful murals on the walls of his basement or on a blank wall on the exterior of their home that might have influenced Pat to pursue painting when living and modeling in New York after college. He had a big Irish laugh and loved to read, tell stories, and have a good time. He was a commercial painting contractor by trade. Before Pat and I married, I needed a job once, and he hired me for a couple days to work for him on a large apartment building. Although he didn't say it, I don't think he thought I was very good at painting. He was a pro.

Nearly eight months into Pat's pregnancy, we were stunned to receive a call from Detroit that her father had suffered a heart attack and had died unexpectedly. He was on heart medication and, like many, especially men, didn't always adhere to the rules taking it. Pat reminded him about his medication every time they talked on the phone.

While eight months pregnant, Pat insisted on flying back to his funeral. I was concerned, but that wasn't going to stop her. The doctor provided careful advice about traveling late in a pregnancy.

***

Things had changed dramatically in childbirth since our daughter had been born in Grand Rapids, Michigan, years earlier. At that time, the hospital didn't allow fathers into the delivery room. I had to wait in the "father's room" while Pat was wheeled into delivery to give birth. This time, in California, with a choice to be in the delivery room or not, I chose to be there.

During her pregnancy, Pat insisted I join her in Lamaze classes each week. I went twice, felt out of place being the only guy there, and didn't go back. She was disappointed, but I assured her I'd read the booklets and would follow the instructions provided.

One morning, at about 1 a.m., Pat shook me awake.

"It's time to go," she said in a soft voice. "My water just broke."

I jumped out of bed and phoned my sister Irene, who lived nearby. She rushed over to stay with Heather.

We grabbed the prepacked hospital bag and left for St. John's Hospital in Santa Monica. We'd practiced driving the route a few times, but that night, the road felt bumpier. My hands were sweating from gripping the steering wheel a little tighter. I must have asked Pat a dozen times during that twenty-five-minute drive, "Are you okay?"

"Yes," she said calmly each time. "I'm fine. Relax." Then I'd hear, "Oh, there's another one." A contraction.

My job during labor was to remind her to breathe and relax, and to be a source of comfort. I failed miserably. My comments didn't seem to help. Neither did the stark labor room with its plain walls, a thin drape, a hospital bed, a bedside table, a single chair for me, and a monitor hooked up to Pat.

A nurse came in from time to time, asking, "How you doing, Mrs. Tar? How long are the contractions?"

Pat wasn't in a talking mood. It wasn't helpful when the doctor came in; looked at the monitor; asked the same question; said, "You're doing just fine"; and vanished out the door.

All I could do was say, "Breathe, relax, breathe."

As the contractions intensified, at one point Pat screamed, "I'm leaving!" and attempted to get up. She quickly fell back with another contraction.

The nurse and doctor returned, examined her, and said, "It's time."

She was wheeled into the delivery room. I followed, feeling quivery and excited at the same time. If the doctor had even the slightest reservation about my being there, I might have left . . . and regretted it, but he didn't. It was surreal. My emotions were on edge, and I was near tears watching the birth of our son, Donovan. My heart was pounding as the nurse handed him to Pat, who, while totally spent, managed a smile. The nurse took a picture of us both with our new son: 11 lbs. 6 oz., nearly the same weight as Heather when she was born.

It was a bit more chaotic at home with a second child competing for our attention. Heather had always been treated like a princess. She had to make some emotional adjustments from being an only child. It wouldn't be easy. She loved bragging to her girlfriends about being a big sister and looked especially proud holding her baby brother. Pat and I had to be mindful of balancing both the kids' needs and our careers. It was important for me to break away from work and spend more time with our growing family, while Pat was determined that her career would not interfere with family. In Hollywood, kids were often pushed to second place. We were determined not to do that.

It was difficult for her to attend last-minute auditions or meet some producer at the drop of a hat. She did audition for a part in the movie *Reds* but didn't get it. One reason, she thought, might have been her height. "Since I'm five-ten," she said, "some shorter male actors are uncomfortable on screen with a taller woman." I don't know if that was the case here, but although she wasn't right for that particular part, Warren Beatty must have seen something in her personality, appearance, or ability because he said he'd mention her to Jack Nicholson.

A couple days later, Nicholson called, wanting to meet her that afternoon. She scrambled for a sitter and drove to meet him at his apartment, a process that took a few hours.

"That's the way it is in Hollywood," she often said. "If you get a call, you're to drop everything and go. They don't want to hear about kids or family either." Pat was thrilled.

How many actresses have the opportunity to talk with Jack Nicholson in a one-on-one about their career?

"He was nice," she told me, still excited, at dinner. "You never know. I presented myself well, he knows who I am now, and maybe there'll be something in the future."

WIN SOME, LOSE SOME

A former Hollywood star was in the White House, and *Star Wars: The Empire Strikes Back* struck big in the movie theaters, as my journey continued.

My RV client handed me another national dealer show to produce as well as a series of additional product films. Despite this, however, I desperately needed to expand my client base. Persistence, hard work, a little luck, and a positive attitude were vital—as well as the stamina to make it through twelve-hour days.

One prospective client I'd been chasing in Long Beach was the *Press-Telegram*, part of the huge Knight Ridder newspaper chain. Like many newspapers, it touted the advantages of advertising in their pages. They made impassioned in-person pitches to agency buyers in New York, Chicago, LA, and elsewhere, potentially resulting in millions and millions of advertising dollars coming their way. My goal was to work with them to produce a fresh, creative pitch they'd use to entice and attract those dollars.

I felt confident talking with newspaper marketing departments, having learned a great deal after producing an award-winning film—and a major show—for the renowned paper the *Detroit News* years earlier. I'd also worked with a group of suburban papers in the Detroit area, helping them with their advertising pitch to buyers. I knew what papers demanded and figured my experience could be an advantage against competitive producers in Southern California who might have little to no interest in how a paper marketed itself.

Steve was head of the paper's promotion department. I made several phone calls to him, hoping to introduce myself, but he was either "in a meeting" or out of the office. One of the most difficult aspects of winning new clients was the tedious job of trying to make the first connection. It was the part of working for myself that I hated the most. I couldn't help but wonder if Steve was simply putting me off.

After a few weeks of trying, I was about to give up, questioning whether it was worth attempting to reach him, when he took my call.

He listened politely as I nervously recapped some of my work and asked for a meeting to tell him more. He had a few questions but didn't respond with much enthusiasm—until I mentioned what I'd done for the *Detroit News*, the largest paper in Michigan. With more audible interest, he pressed for details about what I'd done.

"Tell me a little about what you did," he responded.

"To gain advertisers' attention when the paper was to make its important pitch to them in New York at the Plaza Hotel on Central Park," I said, "we built a thirty-foot stage, four feet high, in the center of the huge ballroom. Directly on it we stacked eight banks of 35mm slide projectors reaching up six feet and a series of colored strobe lights.

We then carefully draped the entire stage and mountain of equipment with polyurethane and let it free-fall on top of the equipment. No matter where anyone stood in the room, they saw this six-foot-high mound of material with pulsating lights beneath."

I heard an "Ah" as he listened. I continued.

"The room was filled with an underlying beat of music as the ad buyers circulated, enjoying drinks and an assortment of food in an elaborate spread. Few paid serious attention to the stage, possibly thinking it was simply the latest creative sculpture of some art director. Then, when the audience least expected it, the room went completely dark, and the tubes that held the poly in place began to fill with air. With changing color strobe lights pulsing, the mass of material began to move and grow in a freeform manner. The two hundred people in the room stood in awe, frozen, watching as the structure became fully erect into a thirty-foot-by-eight-foot-by-eight-foot rectangular theater with eight screens."

"How long did *that* take?" Steve asked.

"About forty seconds," I said. "With everyone's eyes riveted to the stage, the eight screens came alive with a stunning, attention-grabbing, fast-moving, eight-minute presentation on the advantages of buying advertising in the *Detroit News*."

"The total presentation was just eight minutes long?" he asked with a touch of doubt.

"No. It was followed by the paper's vice president of advertising. He had their attention." My adrenalin was pumping as I relived the event. I felt my chest rise, adding, "The New York ad agencies said it was one of the most creative, attention-grabbing presentations they'd seen by a newspaper."

"It sounds dramatic," Steve said.

"It was, and highly successful," I said proudly. "Something national advertisers soon wouldn't soon forget when thinking about a newspaper buy." I took a beat and added, "It was also the featured cover story on *Meetings Magazine*, an industry publication."

He cleared his throat.

"It'll be a couple months before we begin planning our next excursion back east to meet national advertisers," he said, sounding more comfortable than when the phone conversation had begun. "Let's stay in touch as we get closer."

Happy, feeling satisfied he hadn't simply brushed me off, I thanked him.

Over the next month, we briefly talked on the phone a couple times. During those quick calls, he let it slip that he'd been receiving calls from a few other Southern California producers. I didn't say anything, but I was apprehensive. Maybe I was naïve thinking others might not be interested in working with the paper. If I hoped to work with them, I'd better step up my game. I didn't want to make a mistake and miss out, keeping in mind again what the veteran salesperson where I'd worked several years before told me: "Most sales are made after the sixth call, and most people stop calling after the third."

A week later, we set a meeting.

***

The paper's offices took up the entire block at Sixth and Pine in Long Beach. The huge, churning newspaper presses were at street level and could be seen through thick windows by passersby along the street.

Entering the front door, I immediately picked up the subtle aroma of newsprint, powdery and velvet. As I passed closer to the pressroom on my way to Steve's second-floor office, the muffled roaring of presses going full speed issued faintly through the soundproof walls four hallways away.

Steve was friendly, offering a warm smile and firm handshake. He appeared relaxed—his tie was loosened on his white shirt, his sleeves rolled up above the elbows. Even though not a reporter, he had the true look of a newspaperman, and I felt comfortable. Maybe it was because I'd crossed paths with many newspaper reporters while I was a radio/TV journalist. Then again, maybe it was simply that I understood his business.

One wall in his office was filled with cork panels and stick pins holding clippings of newspaper ads, promotions, various banner headlines, and even a couple tear sheets. The small corner table was stacked with what looked like marketing data.

Being comfortable didn't mean I wasn't nervous. I kept reminding myself, *Ed, you don't get a second chance at these meetings. If you don't impress him with what you have to offer, he won't be taking your calls again. Don't waste this opportunity!*

He was a good listener, nodding and acknowledging he was hearing me. We spoke in generalities for a few minutes, feeling each other out. Then he quickly changed the subject to why I was there—his major advertiser presentation. A sense of relief swept through my body. I was anxious to hear about what he had in mind.

He spoke softly and didn't raise his voice, but behind his soft words, he was focused like a laser.

"Our situation is different from the papers you worked with," he said, sitting back, arms crossed. "We're not the dominant paper in the Southern California market like the *News* is in Detroit." He took a deep, cleansing breath. "We're selling our paper's advertising space against the giant up north, the *LA Times*, and a few other locals. Advertisers have a choice!"

"I don't know the numbers," I said, "but imagine you're dominant in the Long Beach market."

He gave an easy nod. "We're challenged to come up with something entirely different every year when we put on our big push with national advertisers. It turns into a dogfight to get our share of national ad dollars against stiff competition."

He shifted his weight, leaning forward in his chair as he reached for a colorful, stiffly heavy chart on his desk. Holding it up, pointing to highlighted areas, he said, "These circulation numbers are good, but unless advertisers think of us, all the numbers in the world won't do any good. We have to remain in the advertiser's mind long after we've left their office."

He shrugged and dropped the chart with a *thud* on his desk.

"We need to get them thinking about us when they shop the Southern California market," he added. "How do we do that?"

Leaning back, resting his hands on the arms of his chair, his chest rising, he looked at me and almost as a challenge said, "I'm open to new ideas. Our presentation will be in the boardrooms of the major ad agencies—no big ballrooms."

I swallowed and shifted in my chair as I asked, "Were you satisfied with what was done in the past?"

"It was okay," he said, "but we need something new."

That wasn't a strong endorsement.

"We need to do something fun, more memorable this time around," he continued.

My heart was pounding.

"I believe I could develop an approach you'd be happy with," I said, holding my breath for his response.

He narrowed his eyes, studying me. "I don't want my boss taking time to sit and listen to the standard presentation."

I sat up straight. "Of course not."

Patience, Ed, I told myself.

With a slight knowing grin, he said, "I'd be open to hearing what you come up with."

"That's great," I replied and felt a thrill move up my spine. "You'll like what I have in mind."

We talked a while longer about what he expected, and the meeting wrapped up.

There was a great deal to do, and I loved it.

***

Three weeks later, a meeting was set in the paper's boardroom for my presentation to Steve, along with the vice president of marketing and advertising, the paper's managing editor, and a member of the sales staff.

They paraded in, and Steve did the introductions. He gave then some background information before giving me the floor. The windowless conference room wasn't large and had a single conference table in the center that could seat about eight people. Copies of their paper sat on a small corner table.

It was tense when I began my presentation and was even more so when I suggested using "magic" to sell the paper to advertisers.

They leaned back, looking skeptical. "Magic?" Steve responded, tilting his head back slightly. I saw uncertainty in his eyes.

The other executives squirmed a little. The editor, looking stern, quipped, "Magic. We could use some." Back and forth glances were exchanged. Eyebrows raised.

I had their attention. Standing there, I continued.

"We'll have a magician be part of your marketing and sales team when making your pitch to national advertisers. He'd be introduced not as a magician but as the newest member of the paper's sales department."

The vice president of sales gave a slight laugh. "That'll be a trick in itself." The others nodded, chuckling softly.

I went on. "He, the magician, will be seated with your salespeople at the conference room table or in the agency's boardroom and actually make part of the pitch. You did say these were smaller rooms."

Steve nodded.

"Dressed in a suit and tie," I said, "he won't appear as the usual plastic-looking magician and will have a rehearsed pitch when it's his turn to talk."

My hands shook a little as I took a sip of water. "He'll say, 'The real reason we're here is that there's money to be made when advertising in the *Press-Telegram.*'"

"There'd better be," chimed in one of the execs at the table, leaning back.

"On the word 'money,'" I said, "his hand reaches into thin air and is suddenly filled with, well . . . money! When he mentions the paper, his other empty hand reaches up, and suddenly a copy of the *Press-Telegram* magically appears in it."

They laughed. I wasn't sure if they thought it was absurd or what. I'd seen many corporate executives clam up whenever something out of the ordinary was presented to them.

"We'll call it *A Little Media Magic.* And he'll continue tying in magic throughout the pitch."

I stopped and turned to Steve. "You wanted something different and memorable. This could be it."

He hesitated, then grinned, adding, "Yes we did."

The others added their own comments about what the magician could say, but no one said, "Let's do it."

It seemed to be going well, but then, niceties don't mean you've got the job. Sales don't always happen in big moments like a pitch; they often happen in little ones when a personal connection is made.

A week later, Steve called and awarded me the contract to move forward.

Bob, who'd written the RV meeting for me, would also write this one. He was an amateur magician himself and knew how magicians think; Bob knew what was possible and what wasn't. He and I screened several magicians at the world-famous Magic Castle in Hollywood, eventually settling on one who was young, personable, and hilarious.

***

Everything went well. The pitch was a hit, and the advertisers were entertained and surprised. It was so effective, the paper used it with advertisers in major markets across the country beyond the big three markets.

Several months later, we produced another major creative media presentation for them, a film called *Advertisers in Paradise*, which was singled out for the top honor by the California Newspaper Advertising Executives Association and also won the Gold Award at the International Film and TV Festival in New York.

***

The *Press-Telegram* was owned by the Knight Ridder newspaper chain. They also owned the San Jose *Mercury News*. My connection with the *Press-Telegram* helped my introduction to the San Jose paper to learn about their media presentation to ad buyers. I reached out and placed a call to Jim, the promotion manager. Although part of the same newspaper chain, the papers were strikingly different in their creative pitch to ad buyers.

San Jose was more conservative. They didn't want a film or a large live presentation. They made one-on-one personal pitches in the ad buyer's office, highlighting marketing data. They wanted a stand-alone, high-quality, tabletop presentation. I thought it was an unexciting way to sell the paper. There was no music, moving images, or emotional dialogue asking for the sale.

I'd never produced any static presentations like this before but offered to show them what we could do for the colorful hardcover presentation they wanted. I used a designer whom I hadn't worked with before to put together a mock-up, and I went up to San Jose to make my pitch.

Meeting in a small, windowless conference room, I carefully presented it to Jim and the vice president of sales.

They were silent as I worked through the pages we designed.

"It doesn't capture our market advantages at all," Jim said. "And it doesn't contain the sophisticated look and feel we want." Looking stern, he added, "We need something much different when making our presentation to tough ad buyers."

A touch of panic raced through my body as I sensed they were about to say, "Thank you but no thanks," and go elsewhere. I humbly asked for the opportunity to make the adjustments and make another more sophisticated mock-up.

There was silence in the room as they looked at each other before Jim said, "Okay," with one caveat. "We need to see it next week."

"Of course," I replied nervously, grateful for a second chance.

The meeting ended. I had my work cut out for me to meet their deadline.

Determined, I called Richard, the creative designer who had done several renderings for me, and asked if he had ever designed anything like what I was looking for. Luckily he had, and he redid the entire design in a more contemporary style, bringing attention to the paper's marketing strengths. The paper loved it.

We wrote and produced the highly sophisticated, colorful, stand-alone, multipage presentation for the paper's individual markets. It was my first time working with a major printing house in Hollywood capable of handling specialized projects. Printing was a whole new medium to learn. Printers have their own language, and not all of them can deliver the level of quality we demanded. I was stressed and uncomfortable through the entire production, but it came together beautifully. I vowed never to do any more work involving large, complicated printing projects.

***

Not every prospective client turned into a success. While on staff at my last job before venturing out on my own, I had worked with one of the large Japanese motorcycle companies and produced their large product introduction show as well as some additional films. I wasn't a cyclist but decided to put that experience to work and contact another large motorcycle company in Southern California.

At the first meeting, with their marketing director and two of his staff members, I should have listened to my gut. The guy couldn't hold eye contact for more than a second when outlining what they were hoping to accomplish at their introduction show. He was shooting from the hip, giving lip service regarding my chances of landing their show.

"Your previous experience really counts with us," he said, speaking in a flat voice. "The fact you are local is a big plus, as is your knowledge of producing shows."

He darted a glance at his assistants, who sat silently. He was flattering me, and I was blinded by it as uncertainty raged in my mind.

Despite my doubtful intuition, I spent a precious amount of time and money putting together a proposal for them. Incorporating some new and unique methods to bring attention to their products, including a large multitiered stage, multiple dramatic product reveals coming in from all sides of the room, lasers (something not seen in corporate shows at the time), multiple giant screen action films, and even 3D, I set a date to meet with them.

During my presentation, the marketing director was joined by two people in his department. The fact that no senior executive was there was a red flag I should have noticed. Usually at least one high-level executive is present in a presentation when a lot of money is being discussed for a major introduction of new products. They were picking my brain with their questions and seemed captivated about the fresh ideas I was presenting, but my gut was not settled. I couldn't escape the fact that the final decision-maker was not in the meeting.

I asked and offered to return to make the same presentation to him, but the marketing director said, "That won't be necessary. I'll tell him about it and give him a copy of your proposal." For me, that sealed it. His words were shallow. I probably wasn't going to get the job.

The show was awarded to their ad agency, who could wrap the show into their ad budget, a corporate practice often designed to deflect some of the real cost of producing a major product introduction. I was disappointed in myself for not seeing through the smoke they were blowing at me.

My experience with them changed my mind about providing free proposals. It also reminded me to listen to my gut.

***

In those early years, I also failed to trust my gut when it came to investing in expensive equipment, assuming equipment would impress clients. I was wrong!

We were renting equipment so often that I decided to purchase multiple high-powered film projectors, a communication system, sound gear, stage drapery, and road cases for everything. Having our own equipment was a bragging point with clients, but it would take more than hardware to win them over.

I purchased expensive controllers that ran individual multitiered projectors, only to find out they were updated so often, I couldn't keep up with the changes. The following year, that piece of equipment was obsolete, and we needed a newer model for the shows we were producing. The old equipment gathered dust in the corner. One of the best decisions I made was to stop buying equipment. It was a money pit. My goal was to create and produce, not to be in the equipment and hardware business.

By this point, it had been almost five years since I'd launched my business and achieved a personal milestone. I had survived the initial demands of working as an independent producer with steady clients.

At home with two growing kids, everything was active. I made it a point to be home for dinner every night.

Pat continued to work on her career and landed parts in various TV series, including *The Mary Tyler Moor Show* and her first feature film role. It remained difficult for her to drop everything on a moment's notice and get into Hollywood for auditions when her agent called.

A NEW OPPORTUNITY

It was time for a change. First, though, I needed more clients. Second, more space.

We'd been in our two small offices since the start. They were confining, especially when a client came in to meet.

I recall thinking when I moved in, *One day it would be great to fill the large suite of offices near the front of the building.*

The thought of moving, with its attendant expense and disruption, was not pleasant. Staying in the current office complex would be perfect, but I didn't see a *For Rent* sign out front. Maybe nothing was available. Early one morning, I saw Irv, the building owner, enter his office across the patio. I decided to pay him a visit. He was alone.

He wasn't surprised to see me as we chatted from time to time about nothing in particular. He and his wife, Sarah, were always open and friendly.

"Morning, Irv," I said. "How you doing today?"

"Uh, fine," he said, sitting at his cluttered desk, holding a steaming coffee mug in his hand. "Want a cup?"

"No thanks."

He took a sip, leaned forward, and set the coffee down. "What's up? What can I do for you?"

"I hesitated to bother you this early," I said, "but something's been on my mind."

He stared at me with a quizzical look. I forced a smile.

"I'm getting a little crowded in my offices. Sarah was right when she told me I'd need more space one day. I was wondering if you had any larger office suites available."

He removed his glasses. "Actually, it just so happens the large front suite might be opening next month. I'm not sure. Sarah will be here in an hour. You can ask her."

The suite had five offices, one large enough to double as a conference room. It was more than double our current space.

Looking satisfied, he reached for his coffee, blew into the cup, and sipped. "Business picking up?"

"Yes. I'm hoping to land another client. Might need to hire a couple people and need more space. I'd like to stay here."

"Well, we'd love to have you stay," he said, sounding sincere. "If you're interested in the front suite, let us know as soon as you can. We've had a few inquiries for space in the last couple weeks."

"Yes! I'm interested. Thanks, Irv."

He took another sip of coffee.

That very afternoon, I talked with Sarah. Sure enough, the offices would be vacant in a few weeks. We came to an agreement on the month-to-month rent, and six weeks later, I moved into larger offices.

***

One of my long-time goals was landing an automotive client. Several years before in Detroit, I worked as a staff producer for a very large media company that sported General Motors as its main client. The company also produced a film I worked on for one of the Japanese car companies in Southern California.

Now living in California, I decided to reach out and make contact with them. The competition was tough. Other more established production companies had long track records with automotive companies. Did I even have a chance? The effort would distract me from the other potential clients I'd been slowly nurturing, but landing an automotive client would signal a major turning point, providing a firm foundation on which to build a bigger, more prestigious clientele list.

Through painstaking doggedness, phone calls, and a couple brief meetings, I slowly built a good relationship with Stu, one of their training managers. He was approachable, friendly, and a true car buff who talked with passion about the car business. He was responsible for providing dealers with the vital information they needed during new product launches and seemed drawn to the fact that I was from Detroit and had experience working on automotive projects, including the film for them a few years earlier.

During our meetings, he'd often go off on a tangent about his passion for classic cars. It had nothing to do with what we were discussing and I knew nothing about them, but not wanting to offend him, I sat and listened. My goal was to win him over as a client without showing any sign of impatience or exasperation.

One time, he invited me to his home for a ride in one of his unusual acquisitions. It was a small, four-door, boxy, tin-looking, rear-engine Volkswagen convertible called the Thing. The top was removable, as were the doors, and the windshield folded down. It had been developed in the 1960s for the West German army and had mild sales success in the US in the '70s. At first glance, it might resemble a toy someone would buy for their kids to play with in the yard. I'd never heard of it but enjoyed listening to Stu enthusiastically brag about it as he took me on a demo ride. We stopped to manually put down the top.

"Want to drive it?" he asked half seriously.

"No thanks. I wouldn't want to damage this . . . thing." We laughed, got back in, and continued on.

Getting to know a client beyond office meetings and business lunches could be a crucial factor in whether you get the job or not. I hoped that would be the case here.

It's difficult when a client is a long distance away, but if they were in town, as this one was, I'd try to get to know them beyond the office.

Since they were closer to home, Pat and I became social friends with Stu and his wife. They lived in Manhattan Beach, a few miles away, and were always gracious and fun. We enjoyed having dinner together a few times at home or out. We had a common non-car interest: we both had four-year-old kids, who seemed to get along when they were together.

***

A few weeks later, I received some good news and was awarded the contract to write and produce a series of 35mm new product filmstrips that were sent to dealers to use in their showrooms. I was thrilled to have landed a giant auto company as a client but was too busy to think about celebrating my triumph.

Over the next eighteen months, we wrote and produced a series of eight filmstrips. It was constant stress as each one contained a different theme, different cars, different talent, and different locations, and they contained most of the ingredients found in producing a live-action film. We wrote the scripts, selected locations, photographed the cars, hired talent, produced the soundtracks, and worked with a large Hollywood film lab to turn out hundreds of duplicates of each. The filmstrips ran at the dealerships on Dukane A-V Matic projection monitors (these were the forerunners of the video monitors that auto dealers eventually switched to). Two of those filmstrips won gold and silver awards at New York's International Film and TV Festival.

We'd been working on the automotive account when my RV client asked us to produce another large dealer show. I was building a solid relationship with the RV executive team and got along especially well with their marketing manager.

The increased volume of work meant I needed more than just freelancers. Monica, my full-time assistant for the past two years, was doing a terrific job running the office. I told her we were about to expand. Holding out as long as possible, always cautious about overhead, I finally hired a full-time production coordinator, Marilyn; a graphics director, Terry; and a customer service person, Carol, who said she could cultivate new business as well.

There were now five of us working together. The responsibility of bringing in enough work for everyone shocked and worried me. I also had to be a referee when disagreements arose, which I never liked. It reminded me of the unpleasant disputes I'd seen when working on staff for my early employers.

***

Successfully completing the series of filmstrips apparently drew the marketing vice president's attention. Gaining it was an important step toward my ultimate goal of one day producing their large new car announcement show, which he was in charge of. Those shows were considered the crème de la crème, the crown jewel of automotive events.

He told Jamie, a promotion coordinator in his department, to call me for assistance on putting together an important presentation he was to make to their dealers. It wasn't a large job, very basic. We'd produce about a hundred carefully hand-designed, high-quality slides/graphics, including car photography, colorful charts, graphs, ads, and titles to support his presentation.

My first meeting with Jamie didn't go well. He was nervous and fidgety, constantly clearing his throat, stumbling over words and rapidly blinking his eyes. I suspected he had limited experience or was simply in over his head, even on this small but important project. His job was to provide us script revisions and internal promotion materials and to arrange the products we'd photograph.

He was in his late twenties, clean shaven, well dressed, six feet tall, and appeared bright. He looked like someone with a corporate future. He frequently demurred, however, when answering questions. With a furrowed brow and a slight smirk, he'd say, "I don't know, maybe. Not sure about that."

Frustrated, I thought, *As the person in charge of this project, you should know.*

As the completion date drew closer, our phone conversations became tense with my cautious reminders: "Time is getting short. We haven't received the needed information and script revisions from you yet."

Jamie would usually respond with "I'm working on it."

Because of the missing information, I suggested changing the completion date.

He cleared his throat. "Can't do that. You'll have to work with what you have."

With a touch of panic in my voice, I replied, "Shouldn't you let your boss know we don't have all the visuals he's expecting to see?"

"I think we'll be okay," Jamie said. "This is only a working session anyway."

I stiffened. *Should I try to contact the head of marketing myself?* That meant going around the coordinator, which could backfire. I decided against it.

The day before our "working session," he dropped a bomb on me: two of the Japanese executives would be in the meeting. They were "shadows," as some referred to them.

Worried, I said, "Do they know we're just working through this, with many holes left to fill?" My experience was they rarely sat in "working sessions."

As expected, his response was hardly reassuring.: "I assume they do."

The next day, the marketing chief and Japanese shadows marched into the large corporate conference room. The two

Japanese men took their seats at one end of the long conference table.

My stomach fluttered. I could feel the tension in the room. Did they know this was incomplete?

The marketing head took his place at a small podium at the front of the room next to the projection screen. He explained how the presentation would be used with dealers.

"Let's get started," he said.

It was a disaster! He didn't expect missing visuals. *Wasn't he told beforehand?*

When he sensed what was happening, the stress level in the room rose exponentially as he quickly moved through his presentation, awkwardly trying to explain the blanks on the screen.

The Japanese executives had expected to see something complete. They mumbled in Japanese to each other, stood up, made a slight bow, said "Thank you," and disappeared.

I was left standing there in the empty conference room with the coordinator and his boss, along with the slight hum of the air conditioner filling the ominous silence.

The marketing head studied his script for a moment and appeared outwardly calm, but underneath I suspected he was livid about looking unprepared, especially in front of the Japanese executives. He looked up, first at the Jamie, who stood there with his eyes blinking rapidly, then at me. Glowering, he asked for an explanation.

"My understanding was this was only going to be a working session with the three of us," I said nervously.

He turned to Jamie, who was trembling, trying to explain the missing materials.

"They shouldn't have seen this until it was completed," the marketing head said, sounding annoyed. "When will the holes be filled?"

"As soon as the agency sends us the material," Jamie responded. "I'll call them this morning."

Grabbing his rumpled script, the marketing chief got up, hung a pen in his shirt pocket, peered at Jamie with narrowed eyes, and said sternly, "See me in my office immediately when this room is cleared."

He didn't say a word to me and walked out. I was crushed and disappointed in myself for not being more aggressive about my concerns.

Over the next several days, we filled the empty holes. But that was the last project they asked me to do. All my work building that relationship went up in flames.

It's a very slow process to land a client but a very quick one to lose it.

I talked with Stu about what had happened and asked for advice about what to do to regain their trust. He didn't offer much. I suspect his mind might have been on other things.

For me, it was a hard lesson to learn: Be sure you have direct access to the decision-maker. Without it, you may be wasting your time waiting for others to decide what to do. And it could affect your own job and career.

Also, never break the golden rule: *Make your clients look good in front of their superiors*. I never forgot it.

***

Feeling like a failure, I took my depression home with me.

Pat, ever the positive person, told me everything was going to be alright. "We have each other and two beautiful children," she said, trying to be her usual supportive self.

Yet between the long days, little sleep, and much stress, work was getting the best of me. I was getting angry for no reason at all. We were arguing more, and it was uncomfortable when the kids heard us.

Following dinner one night, after the kids had gone to bed, Pat said we ought to go to a "marriage encounter weekend," where they would tell us how to get in touch with each other.

"No way," I adamantly responded, raising my voice. "We don't need to spend a weekend listening to some stranger lecture us. It's a waste of time and money."

I slammed the refrigerator door shut. Pat stood across the kitchen with a dour look on her face.

"Look, let's give it a try," she said. She took a step toward me. "If we don't like it, we can leave. They say the weekend is about getting to know each other more."

"I *already* know you," I said.

Her reply was swift. "No you don't!"

That stunned me. "What do you mean? Of course I do."

"Look, I think a weekend alone would do us good," she persisted.

I slowly gave in.

Two weeks later, we were sitting with about a dozen other couples, mostly over thirty-five years old, in a small dull-looking hotel meeting room, listening to someone tell us about intimacy and getting to know each other again.

"Take a look at the person you came here with," the lecturer said. "Tell them at least one thing you like about them."

I thought it was silly and, looking at Pat, blurted out, "I love your smile and your enthusiasm."

She smiled—fittingly—and said, "I love you, your eyes, your voice, your kindness, and everything about you."

That made me feel good.

Before we knew it, we had forgotten about time and became fully engaged in the weekend, sharing our feelings with each other.

We didn't interact much with the other couples who were there. Other than a morning and afternoon group session where the lecturer was encouraging us to try new techniques to strengthen our marriage, we spent most of our time together applying what he said into practice.

Pat was right. We became closer that weekend, expressing our love for each other both verbally and in notes the moderator insisted we write and read to one another. We held hands nearly all weekend. It also helped, me in particular, to focus on what's important in a marriage and a family.

***

Losing the automotive business was a huge disappointment, but all was not lost. It freed me to focus my attention on more business from my RV client and to search for new clients.

Stu, whom I had worked well with on the filmstrips, had moved over to another Japanese car company. My hope for a large automotive client was reborn. It wasn't long before he gave us the opportunity to videotape the live finals of a nationwide sales competition they were conducting in Los Angeles. They were pleased with how it turned out, and I was happy with my team, who worked so hard to make it a success.

Several weeks later, Stu said they needed to videotape a short statement by one of their top executives to be released to dealers. It was basic and required minor editing. He told me to contact their advertising agency. They were handling the bid process. I did and submitted a bid.

Three weeks went by, and hearing nothing, I called them. They said the project had been given to the same production company that produced their expensive TV commercials. They told me something I'd never heard before: "Your price was low. We weren't sure how you could do it for the price quoted."

My mistake. I hadn't explained the details enough and assumed everyone knew it wouldn't cost much to do.

I enjoy working directly with a client, not an in-between such as an ad agency. Ray, on the other hand, often liked working directly with the agency.

***

At about the same time, I sent samples of my work to the government's procurement office in Washington, DC, asking to be put on the US government's "preferred producer list." If accepted, I would be invited to bid on films needed by various government departments and agencies. Also, it could impress potential corporate clients. Several weeks later, I received the letter approving me as a government preferred producer. I was happy.

Shortly after, I received the first request for a bid on a complicated film, to be shot at the Redstone Arsenal in Alabama. The bid request was filled with pages and pages of detailed questions about the background of each crew member, what they'd be paid, estimated number of hours, details about equipment to be used, insurance details, and so forth. I'd never had to provide so many details on corporate films.

It took several days to complete the bid, and I anxiously submitted it. A few weeks later, they notified me the film had been awarded to the same people they'd used before. My bid had probably been a waste of time.

A few months later, the US Postal Service sent a lengthy bid request for a series of training films. As we were just about to submit the meticulously prepared bid, they sent me multiple pages of revisions, basically a complete redo. Rather than continue devoting a great deal of time preparing bids and with no personal contact with the government employee dispatching bid requests, I sent a letter to them asking to be removed as a preferred producer. It wasn't an easy decision, but I didn't have the mindset to deal with bureaucracy.

VENICE BEACH

Perseverance may have been one reason for my early success, but working with the best people, delivering creativity and quality, and keeping dreams alive were equally important. My urge to stay on the leading edge and to make any and all necessary changes constantly occupied my mind. With an expanded staff, I again needed additional office space.

In my business, every penny had to be spent with a good reason. An internal debate raged within me: Was it better to own my office or keep paying rent? Could I afford to own? How would owning help business? Should I talk to a real estate agent? Interest rates were still very high following the Carter years in the White House.

Maybe I should just stay where I was. Irv and Sarah, my landlords, had always been supportive and helpful.

No, I told myself, it's time to move on. Remain calm. You can do this.

Well—is this happening or not?

My sister Irene, who had moved to California from Detroit a few years before me, was a real estate agent in Los Angeles. She was married and had no children. Her husband, Clark, was also a real estate agent. We'd visit and talk frequently. I mentioned my thoughts about owning my own office rather than continuing to pay rising rent. Irene was confident she could locate a small, affordable property for me. Aware of tightness in my chest, I took a deep breath and gave her the go-ahead with the stipulation that it had to be in West LA.

For the next couple months, in between my meetings with production crews and clients, we began looking at real estate options. Over a period of several weeks, we checked out a dozen possibilities. It was frustrating until, at last, Irene found a small single-story duplex in Venice, two blocks from the beach. It had possibilities.

Pat and I talked about my moving, but the Venice location was a surprise. She was 100 percent behind it. We loved the creative vibe Venice gave off.

Known worldwide for its famous boardwalk, Muscle Beach, and laid-back style, and for nurturing whole generations of Beat and hippie poets, artists, and writers, Venice had never entered my mind. Behind some of those unmarked doors lived some of Hollywood's best-known stars, agents, and producers.

The weathered duplex looked like many others built in the late forties and early fifties. It didn't present well but had potential—if we could get it for the right price.

It needed new paint and a new roof. There was a broken forty-year-old chain-link fence in front and a termite-infested wooden fence in the rear. With a door broken beyond repair, the attached single-car garage proved useless.

The musty interior needed a complete remodel, but I envisioned how it could turn into seven or eight offices. It was more space than I currently had. Turning it into working offices meant more expense, something I fought hard to control. The debate within me continued: Should I look at something with fewer problems and less expense? My gut said this was a good investment as my mind kept wandering to a worst-case scenario.

We made a low offer.

Things moved quickly for a couple days, back and forth with counters, until we reached an agreement. When Irene called me with the news they had accepted our last offer, I sat back at my desk, closed my eyes, and took a deep breath. Letting my breath escape into the warm, thick air, I realized I'd just become the owner of my own office—a significant and pivotal turning point.

A contractor came in, and we practically gutted the insides, knocking down walls and adding a door between each unit in the duplex and also the attached garage. We removed closets, appliances, sinks, and floor coverings and turned what were bedrooms and two kitchens into offices. We replaced the old fences with wrought iron and converted the garage into a graphics studio.

With the remodeling expenses mounting, I had to keep reminding myself: this was an investment, better than continuing to pay rising rent.

***

Feeling happy, though not without a touch of sadness about leaving Irv and Sarah, I gave them my thirty-day notice. During the over five years I was with them, they'd seen many tenants come and go, and were not terribly surprised to see me move on. Their friendship and support had meant a great deal. They gave me free additional parking, free use of their storage shed, and free maid service from time to time, and they allowed me to use additional office space when needed without charging for it.

Sarah was her usual positive self. "We're going to miss you," she said.

I handed her my office keys and gave her a hug. "I'll miss you too," I said, "and will stop by to say hello when in the neighborhood."

Irv stood in the same doorway as the day we met. Seemingly impatient—though I sensed he was covering up his emotion—he said, "Okay. . . . Yes. . . . Stop by. Okay. . . . Fine. Thank you."

I reached out and shook his hand. He broke eye contact and turned his forward-leaning body toward his desk. He sat down and glanced out the window onto the patio as he always did when deep in thought.

***

In my own building with a staff of five, each with their own office now, there was a new energy.

Adding to the spirited feeling, Pat brought over a couple of her latest abstract paintings to hang. Between her TV and film acting roles and two children at home, she continued to spend time behind her easel creating exciting and vibrant oil and acrylic works, some of which would be exhibited in galleries and museums internationally.

Despite everything else going on, I was having trouble with my customer service person, Carol. When hired, she said she would bring in new clients. In the year she'd been on staff, however, she appeared more content offering advice on clients we already had than reaching out to new ones. Carol was being paid well with full benefits and wasn't delivering on her guarantee. Also, from day one, she was having difficulty getting along with Monica, my assistant and office manager, preferring to act as her boss rather than a coworker.

I couldn't afford friction or her inactivity and made the agonizing decision to let her go. It was difficult. She was the first person I'd ever fired. Monica was relieved, and I sensed Marilyn and Terry were also. Carol seemed to get under everyone's skin.

My production coordinator, Marilyn, was aggressive and doing a super job dealing with the various film crews, labs, film locations, and other production challenges. She also worked well with Terry, my graphics director, who was more laid back. He'd been working for me for the last two years.

Business was changing and growing. We had a couple steady clients who stuck with us. I believe it was because of the personal attention and service we gave them. I was determined to make that personal touch a hallmark of what I did.

Meanwhile, large competitors, sporting staffs of fifty or more and a warehouse full of equipment, continued grabbing some of the larger shows and productions, leaving midsize competitors with maybe half that many people grappling to stay afloat.

An old pro in the business gave me some early advice I'd never forget: "Either become very large or stay very small. If you find yourself in the middle in this business, your expenses will go up exponentially, and in the long run, you'll struggle to survive."

Going forward, I made a pivotal decision to work as a small, boutique producer rather than attempt to grow large and simply slam out productions. I'd seen the other way, and it was not fulfilling to worry about overhead, a large staff, and all that came with it. I liked the freedom to pick and choose what to do and who to work with.

I had strong relationships with writers, directors, editors, and other creative people specifically experienced for the job at hand, and I wouldn't be forced to accept projects just to make a big payroll.

A few large potential clients had trouble with the idea of using a small independent producer.

I invited two senior executives from a corporation to my new offices to tell them about what we did. They were searching for someone to produce their annual show for franchisees. I made my presentation about the shows and meetings we produced as they sat quietly in the small conference room. I was nervous and sensed trouble when one of them asked, sounding skeptical and crossing his arms, "How do you produce the shows and meetings you say you do out of these small offices with a limited staff?"

I'd heard that question before, and tried to reassure him we did, offering to provide the names of the individuals at the companies we worked with, but they weren't comfortable. Two weeks later, I called them and was told they were going to use a larger producer. They didn't give me an opportunity to submit a bid.

It took me a while to understand it, but after wandering the corridors of corporate America for the past several years, I'd come to the realize that some corporate executives only felt comfortable working with layers of people. It's what they knew. That was fine, but it wasn't me, and I had no intention of hiring a lot of people.

But I soon learned I was hardly too small for the likes of the IRS.

STEPPING INTO TV

"Try to avoid doing anything that would attract IRS attention," my longtime accountant, Steve, had drilled into my head whenever I called him with a question about taxes. "Even when doing everything by the book, the IRS can find something to question you about."

It was with a jolt when I turned over an envelope I'd received in the mail and saw it was from the IRS. Just seeing those all-serious, bureaucratic words *Internal Revenue Service* made my stomach quiver. Staring at it for a moment, I took a breath before my finger moved under the flap of the envelope to slowly open it and pull out the letter. "*Your Federal Tax Return has been selected for examination*" popped off the page.

Those are words no one wants to hear, or read, and it was the first time they'd been directed at me. After glancing over the letter, I reached for the phone to call Steve.

"I just received a letter from the IRS," I told him. "They want to do an 'on-site' tax examination." I read him the list of documents they had asked to see.

He didn't sound ruffled, but his voice took on a serious tone. "Send me a copy of the letter. Let me review it and get back to you."

Steve—whom Pat and I had met in Detroit years earlier—had been doing our personal and business taxes for a long time and knew everything about us financially. He lived in La Jolla, just north of San Diego. He was financially conservative and soft-spoken, and he had the uncanny, and useful, ability to enter a room totally unnoticed.

He called back a few days later. "I'll contact them and confirm a time to meet," he told me. "I'll come up to LA the day before the audit to lay everything out, including the latest ledgers and financial statements. You shouldn't be in the office during the audit. In fact, make it a point not to be."

His voice was calm as he had been through this before. He knew the routine.

I was anxious, my leg bouncing up and down. "Why shouldn't I be here?"

"It's easier for me to defer answering the auditor's questions, saying I need to talk with you first for an answer."

"But you're the one who prepared the statements," I chimed in. "Doesn't that matter?"

"Of course it does, but I prepared them from information you provided. Your not being in the office will give us time to double-check our response before answering."

Steve came to the office the day before, as he said, and meticulously lined up the requested documents on the conference room table. I stood there as he huddled over the table like a painter putting the final touches on a masterpiece and remarked, "It looks like you're doing all the detail work for them." He grinned. "When the auditor comes in, it's important he see a well-organized, easy-to-find set of documents." He continued adjusting a few papers, putting a title page on each set. "I'll walk him through everything and answer any questions."

The day of the audit, I was out of the office visiting my RV client in Riverside, who I hoped didn't notice my distractedness.

Before heading back late that afternoon and with my mind aflame with worst-case scenarios, I called the office. Steve was still there.

"How's it going?" I asked nervously.

"We finished, and it went well," he said, sounding confident.

A sense of relief swept through my body.

"The auditor left an hour ago. I'm packing up. He questioned some expenses and a small amount of retained earnings. I assured him you needed cash to immediately begin a production as clients don't often pay quickly. I also mentioned the possibility of investing in some video equipment."

"I'm not going to invest in equipment," I quickly interrupted. "It changes so fast, it'd be outdated by the time I got to use it."

"I know, I know," he answered, "but you could change your mind, and besides, you need funds if there's a business downturn."

"You're right about that."

"The auditor was young, and I guided him through what to look for on the ledgers. He appreciated how easy it was to locate everything. You don't owe them anything."

My chest felt lighter. "That's great! Thank you, Steve."

Three weeks later, another letter arrived from the IRS. This time I opened it quickly. It confirmed the audit was complete, with no further contact needed. Phew.

***

It was the mid-eighties. The world, with all its problems, opportunities, and changes, continued to turn. The PC had marched onto the scene, arcade games had blown up, and channels like MTV, CNN, Nickelodeon, and other cable networks were flooding American living rooms. Shopping shows were a popular and successful format as companies jumped at having their products exposed on TV.

My small staff was concentrating on the corporate work we were doing and had it all under control. I was looking for a new challenge and wanted to branch out into something other than corporate shows and videos.

For the past few years, I had been producing videos for my RV client, weaving in stories and active lifestyle scenes about the enjoyment of owning an RV and the experience of traveling to a destination in one of their products.

In the back of my mind, I couldn't escape thinking, *These videos would be perfect as part of a travel show on cable TV. They're complete and with some editing could easily be adjusted to work in a TV format.* A crazy idea struck me. *Why not produce a TV show yourself using the RV videos?*

The last TV show I had produced was as a journalist, working for a television station in Michigan.

The current TV shows about travel didn't excite me. My vision was a program about the destination and also the excitement of getting there. An RV was only one way. I'd title it *Getting There and Enjoying It.*

With no funding, I was uncertain how to venture into TV on my own. *There are destination and travel bureaus everywhere. I bet they'd be happy to supply us free destination film footage. It'd save me money rather than having to send film crews on location.*

I mentioned the idea to Pat. She was very supportive, as she always was, and even more so when I told her, "You could be the on-camera host."

She especially liked that there'd be no auditions. She'd been to enough of those and had received her fill of rejections.

With her TV experience, she'd be the perfect host for the show. Pat worked with producers in Hollywood but in front of the camera acting. She couldn't offer much help with whom I might contact for assistance with the development or financing. Besides, everyone in Hollywood had an idea or a script, and I'd be just another one in the crowd.

I'd worked with a few travel-related clients—automobiles, motorcycles, and RVs—that might be interested in participating as sponsors, maybe buying short segments to feature their products, but the list had to be expanded.

I traveled to Florida and met with cruise lines and to New York for meetings with a couple ad agencies and travel clubs. The response was the same with everyone: "It's sounds interesting, but no thanks until we see a program."

Trying to line up potential sponsors, I felt somewhat out of my league having never sold advertising or sponsorships before.

I turned to TV distributors in L.A. and New York. They offered advice, but none were eager to jump into a relationship with an unknown producer with no track record. The ones who showed an interest asked to see a finished pilot.

Discouraged at failing to get any financial support from distributors and sponsors, I agonized about writing and producing a pilot, paying for it myself.

Closer to home, I set a meeting to explain my idea to my RV client. There was tension in the room as Earl, head of the RV division, and Larry, the marketing manager, sat listening stoically during our meeting. I outlined the concept and benefits they could reap buying a segment on the program to showcase their products. They'd been a good, steady client.

"How would our products be positioned?" Earl asked cautiously, leaning back in his chair. "What will they look like? What will be said?"

Encouraged by their questions, my heart beat faster. "We'll create wonderful stories about the fun and enjoyment traveling to a favorite vacation spot in one of your products," I told them.

They perked up a bit but were hesitant to commit any money at the time. "Let us think about it," Earl said with a glance at Larry. "Give us a call next week."

Anxiously, I placed the call, and after answering a few more questions, they agreed to come aboard—under one condition. I needed to secure a commitment from a cable network to air it before they would buy into the pilot and possibly additional shows with different products in each one.

***

My general knowledge about the TV industry had to improve quickly, and I needed more contacts.

There was a television convention about to take place in New Orleans. All the networks, including cable and TV station managers from across the country, would be there. I decided to take a few days away from my daily work with corporate clients and go. Pat was all for it. It would be a perfect opportunity to see the main players in the business all in one place.

As I walked into the convention hall the first morning, my senses came alive. It was bustling with activity and energy. Presentation booths for networks, studios, and distributors covered at least a couple hundred thousand square feet of space, many equipped with TV monitors showing the programs they were producing. Slick brochures sat on tables as wide-smiling sales reps greeted those who stopped to peruse. The air vibrated with laughter, music, schmoozing, and hype. The smell of fresh coffee and cinnamon buns filled various distributor booths.

Rather overwhelmed, I stood there for a moment, taking it all in.

With a deep breath, I tightened my hold on my small briefcase—which had the broad script I had written for the pilot—and waded into the action. I had no preset meetings and knew no one there.

Everyone wore a badge. Station managers, the most important people in the eyes of the distributors, wore red ones. Media folks wore white. And the rest of us wore blue.

Walking slowly past distributor booths, I eyeballed what they were pitching, asking myself, *Would they be interested in my show?* Somewhat intimidated by all the hype and activity, I welled up my courage, stopped into a booth of a well-known television distributor, and asked for a moment of their time to tell them about the show. They were busy but listened, more out of courtesy than any real interest, as I made my brief elevator pitch.

"We're not taking on any new shows, but stay in touch" was a standard answer I heard throughout the day.

I picked up the vibe. They preferred talking with big-time producers with track records who had money and shows already under their belt. They also catered to the TV station managers. Couldn't blame them for any of that, and I soon began questioning what I was doing there.

My confidence was low when I walked into the large booth for SPN, the Satellite Program Network (not to be confused with ESPN). Nervous amid the busy display, I struck up a conversation with a guy who was standing there looking relaxed, observing the goings-on around him. His name was Eric, and he was a producer about to launch his own shopping show on SPN. He had a friendly smile and confident manner. I mentioned the show I was planning, and he pointed out various people in the booth to talk with about it.

Just then, Jerry, the head of network programming, casually walked up, wearing a wide grin. He looked to be in his late forties and wore a plain dark blue suit with a white shirt and tie, similar to the uniform of many on the convention floor. Behind his dark-rimmed glasses, his eyes were wide.

He reached out his hand to say hello to Eric, whom I had been talking with. They knew each other.

Then Eric generously introduced me. "Jerry," Eric said, "Ed was telling me about a new program he's producing. Sounds interesting."

"Nice to meet you," Jerry said, reaching out his hand to shake. "Where you from, Ed?"

"LA," I said.

"LA. I know it well. Used to live there a few years ago."

"Oh? Whereabouts?"

"Burbank," he answered, his eyes darting around as others kept coming up to interrupt and say hello. "So, what've you been working on? Tell me a little about it."

"It's a travel and adventure series called *Getting There and Enjoying It*," I began, but after a moment of constant interruptions, it was impossible to maintain a focused conversation.

"Mind if we go somewhere we can talk?" he suggested, gesturing to a curtained area in the back of the booth.

"Not at all." I felt important with a burst of confidence.

I exchanged departing pleasantries with Eric, then followed Jerry to a couple chairs.

For the next twenty minutes, I anxiously outlined what I was working on. I was nervous, hoping he wouldn't abruptly end our conversation, but he seemed to like the concept, nodding at certain points. He was particularly interested in how I intended to produce the programs before addressing my background and experience.

"If the pilot turns out as you're describing"—he shifted in his chair—"we'll take a look at it."

Crossing his legs and sitting back, looking confident, he continued, "Only after seeing the pilot would we consider airing it and then talk about the possibility of additional shows."

That's what I was hoping to hear. I took it as an auspicious beginning.

Our eyes locked, as if waiting for the other to continue.

With a satisfied smile, I said, "Understood. Fair enough."

A feeling of contentment filled me. With a commitment from a cable network—even though it was contingent on seeing a pilot—it would be easier to approach potential sponsors.

"Keep me abreast of how the pilot is going," he said, smiling, as we stood up and shook hands. "I look forward to seeing it."

My concentration had been so strong talking with him, the noise and activity around us was tuned out. Now, lost in reverie for a few minutes, happy and relaxed, I lingered. A thought crossed my mind: *Is it time to run the music?* New doors were about to open.

***

With a network commitment, or at least the promise of one, I returned to my RV client. They bought a segment on the pilot. I was able to land another very small travel company to buy in. Together, they brought in enough money to just about cover the basic cost of writing and producing the pilot with stories about the fun and adventure in getting to unusual destinations.

I sent the finished pilot to SPN. They liked what they saw. We talked back and forth on the phone and came to an agreement about the number of future episodes. SPN followed through on their commitment to air the pilot and the entire series of thirteen half-hour programs we produced.

Pat was a wonderful and beautiful host on all the shows, weaving together the stories we were telling. To add more audience appeal, we brought in celebrities to tell us where they escaped to out of the spotlight.

Actor Marty Kove revealed his enjoyment going to Jackson Hole, Wyoming, to explore where the Hole in the Wall Gang had roamed a hundred years ago. Game show host Art James, a pilot, said he'd fly a small plane to some out-of-the-way spot with a small runway where he could set it down. "Even if I'm just going to grab lunch," he added.

Other celebrities and people in the know added their own stories about travel adventures.

The first show received a huge lift when Gerry, a friend who was the editor of a large television weekly magazine reaching decision-makers across the country in television advertising, made me a very generous offer. He'd run a complimentary full-page color ad about the show in a coming edition if we would send him completed artwork. We did and he did. It was exciting to see. It provided vital exposure and credibility when pursuing potential sponsors for the show.

The show was honored with an award at the International Film and TV Festival in New York. Pat and I flew to accept the award. It was a thrill for both of us. With New York traffic and all, we missed most of the dinner but arrived in time to receive the award.

The programs brought in some money from the cable network but not enough to continue devoting a great deal of my or my small staff's time to independent TV production. Fortunately, my reliable corporate clients were keeping us busy with live events, videos, and films. It was only because of the money I was earning from them that I was able to survive the TV venture. They deserved my full attention.

Even though the show was an award winner, producing it taught me to be cautious venturing into areas where I had limited experience and contacts.

***

During the New Orleans convention, I was struck by a stark reminder of something I'd experienced previously. They held an easy 5K race one morning for convention-goers before doors opened in the convention hall. Even though I'd never run in any race before, I decided to give it a try. Some TV distributors I had hoped to meet were taking part, and I thought it'd be a good conversation piece back on the convention floor.

The run was fine, but walking back to the hotel a couple blocks away, I began to feel weak and faint. A rash of giant red welts covered my body. I entered my room and collapsed on the bed. My mind was racing. *Why was this happening? Again!* I dozed off.

My body calmed an hour later, after which I called my doctor in LA. He didn't know of my previous episode with this.

"Maybe you touched something or ate something that didn't agree with you," he proffered. "If it happens again, go to the ER. Come see me when you're back home."

He wasn't very reassuring.

With a family, employees, and clients counting on me, I refused to dwell on something as simple as dizziness, weakness, and rashes. It was probably just exhaustion.

MOVING TOWARD THE LIGHT

I had no time for doctors.

For their new product launch, my RV client had just asked me to write and produce a dozen product videos, each fifteen to twenty minutes long. With less than five months from start to finish, the timeline was a killer. However, as a small producer with flexibility, I relished the challenge.

Fortunately, I had a small staff plus a cadre of reliable freelance writers, cameramen, and video editors ready to work. There were a half-dozen writers whom I'd used the past few years I could call on. Each had their own style and way of interacting with a client for script material. Some sat quietly taking notes; others craved back-and-forth dialogue.

My writer friend Bob, a seasoned pro, knew the client from the other scripts he'd written for them and was my first choice. He always delivered quality work on time and never rushed when talking. Bob, the pipe smoker, paused often to meticulously pack, light, or clean his pipe. I think it was his way of collecting his thoughts.

I also hired Joe once again, a fresh, eager young writer who'd done a great job on a previous film we'd produced for an oil company. At the time, he used a relatively new tool to take notes at client meetings: a laptop. It made me feel good, bringing in someone who utilized the latest tools.

Then there was George, a Harvard Business graduate. I'd received his résumé in the mail months earlier and had simply placed it in the file. I couldn't envision a Harvard grad writing product videos, but because of the volume of work on this job and his other corporate writing credits, I decided to give him a shot. It helped that he lived in LA, so we could meet often.

While a very direct and terrific writer, George was not fond of rewriting. To help keep it to a minimum, he often repeated instructions and meticulous product information the client provided to eliminate mistakes and redoing anything.

Three cameramen carried the load on this and other productions. Al, who I'd known and worked with since my days in Detroit, was my go-to guy. He'd flown out often to LA to shoot RVs and cars for me. He was excellent under pressure. Al never raised his voice and methodically shot a scene from every angle, making sure we had enough footage beyond what was in the script. He had a calm approach, and the video crew loved working with him, even when the temperature outdoors was nearing one hundred degrees and tempers sometimes flared as we jockeyed RVs around in the heat.

My second cameraman, Mike, had also shot for me before. He was top-notch, having worked on many large-scale TV and feature films. He knew to shoot enough footage to make the editor's life easier, as did Paul, my third cameraman, who was creative, quick and flexible.

We shot with a small crew that moved quickly, and it meant everyone shouldered more than one job. Al, Mike and Paul often reset the camera themselves or adjusted a light or reflector. Those tasks on big Hollywood shoots usually fell to grips and assistants.

I was grateful they were available for the five weeks we shot on location around Southern California in state parks, at lakes, and on various state and county roads. We also shot at the client's manufacturing facilities in Riverside.

Setting up serene lifestyle scenes with on-camera talent enjoying their RV in a park or at a lake was more enjoyable and less dangerous than filming RVs moving down the road. The various road shots required close radio communication and coordination between the driver of the RV and the driver of the camera car as well as the cameraman. It took more time, even when we had police often holding traffic. We shot over a dozen large RVs on several different roads and highways.

When it came time to edit, the TV industry was fortunately on hiatus during the summer, meaning editors and Hollywood editing facilities needed work. Merv Griffin's TAV, a video facility near Sunset and Vine, was anxious for us to come there. They gave us great rates and two of their top-notch creative editors who worked on some of TV's biggest hit shows, which thrilled me. We developed a close working relationship, though the stress of getting everything done always hung over my head.

It was intense and exhausting to sit next to the editor in an editing bay for eight hours, then back to the office for another couple hours of reviewing scripts and shot lists to plan the next day's edit.

Often, my answer to shedding that stress was to turn to the ice rink to play hockey. Although Pat was very understanding, I sensed she sometimes resented my going to the rink, leaving her alone with the kids in the evening after she had been with them all day. The tension level rose at home.

***

The closest ice rink near home was in downtown Santa Monica. Built in 1966 and operated by Ice Capades Chalet, it was a popular gathering place for public skaters, figure skaters, and amateur hockey games. It was even featured in the first *Rocky* movie, when Stallone's titular character decides to ask Adrian on a date and they go ice-skating.

Playing hockey there had its challenges. The ceiling was very low, and a 1960s disco-style mirror ball hung above the ice. There was no protective glass for spectators, and players' benches were butted up against a cinder block wall painted with outdoor snow scenes.

Two very small locker rooms flanked the ice, neither with showers. A small skate rental shop and an old-style snack bar completed the picture. The rink hadn't been updated in nearly twenty years, but we didn't care as long as the ice was good.

One night, playing in a game with our regular group of guys, my body lacked energy, my mind was foggy, and my equipment felt heavier than normal. It had been a very long day for me that had begun at five thirty that morning.

As the game moved on, my skin under the pads on my legs, arms, and shoulders began crawling and itching. Heat and sweat poured out of my body. My hands were swollen and red.

Skating to the players' bench, I frantically pulled off my jersey, hoping for some relief. It didn't help. I began yanking off my shoulder pads.

I didn't see them arrive, but two paramedics pushing a gurney and carrying red medic cases were quickly directed to the players' bench, where they knelt over a limp body, shirtless, lying there. It was me.

I was floating above the bench, being pulled toward a warm bright light. Calm and smiling, I said, *Relax. Everything's going to be okay.* They didn't respond. I didn't feel anything but serenity and peacefulness as the light intensified. I was no longer in the limp body.

One of the paramedics opened the emergency medical kit as the other paramedic asked what had happened.

"We don't exactly know," a player said. "He came off the ice to the bench and for some strange reason frantically removed his equipment before collapsing."

A small, hushed crowd of sweating players in hockey gear, some without helmets and holding their sticks, stood watching. They exchanged glances. What words they expressed were in low, hushed tones. Spectators from the other side of the rink took notice of the commotion.

Working quickly, the paramedics went into action. "He has a weak pulse," one of them said in a calm voice.

"His body temperature is dropping. Start the IV." He reached for the syringe from the medical kit. "Use the left arm."

He quickly attached the tubes and bag, which would carry the vital fluid into my unresponsive body. They pulled the gurney closer and unbuckled the straps that lay across the top, letting them dangle off the side as they removed the blanket.

As I watched, I said, but no one heard me, *Why are you concerned? Don't be. Everything's going to be fine. Take your time. If you could be where I am, you would understand there's nothing to worry about.*

***

The paramedics carefully lifted the limp body onto the gurney, covering it with a blanket and quickly fastening the straps around it.

The players watched. One of them asked, "Is he going to be okay? What hospital are you taking him to?"

"Santa Monica Medical Center," a paramedic replied.

In a flash, I was yanked from that warm, bright light and landed back on the gurney as my eyes blinked open. I was being wheeled toward a waiting ambulance.

As we began driving to the hospital, a paramedic sat next to me, watching a monitor. Confused, I opened my eyes again and muttered, "What happened?"

"You passed out," he said. "Your body temperature and pulse dropped dangerously low."

My head still foggy, I said, "I was in such a bright, warm, peaceful place, but . . ."

"When the IV kicked in, you regained consciousness," he said. "It brought you back."

I'm not sure I wanted to come back, I thought and closed my eyes.

Siren blaring, the ambulance sped to the hospital several blocks away. I felt tired as we pulled up to the emergency entrance and the gurney was wheeled through the hospital doors. I was embarrassed. Emergency is only for people who have been in car crashes or who were shot or had suffered heart attacks, not for someone like me who had simply passed out. There were people who had more serious issues.

We stopped for a brief moment at the emergency desk as the paramedics gave a ten-second version of what was going on. We were directed to a small room, where the middle-aged nurse in her light blue hospital uniform offered instructions. A very young, slightly overweight orderly was with her. He didn't say anything.

"Relax, Mr. Tar," the nurse said. "We're going to move you off the gurney."

"Oh, I can do that myself," I said, attempting to sit up.

"Mr. Tar, just lie still for a moment," she said with a sharp tone. The paramedics and orderly moved closer and took hold of my body. "Okay, up you come. Take it slow." She handed me a white hospital gown with an open back. "Let's see if we can slip this on."

The IV bag was removed, but the small insertion tube in my arm with a clip on it was left in in case they had to start it again. She took my blood pressure, temperature, and oxygen level. The room was cold and smelled sterile. I had a quick flashback to the sterile hospital room where my father died.

I asked for a blanket. A bank of hospital equipment sat ready to be put to use. The paramedics left. The nurse remained, asking rapid-shot questions.

"How are you feeling now, Mr. Tar?"

"Okay," I said.

"You passed out. Has that happened before?"

"No."

"Do you have any allergies?"

"No."

"Are you taking any medications or drugs? Allergic to any medications?"

"No. None."

A few minutes later, a very young doctor came in wearing his hospital scrubs with his name tag on the front and a coiled stethoscope in his side pocket. He glanced at the chart the nurse handed him. She described what the paramedics had said, and he turned to me with more questions.

"How you feeling, Mr. Tar?"

"I'm feeling fine."

"Let's see what's going on with you. It says here your blood pressure dropped dangerously low and you're breathing nearly stopped. Has that ever happened before?"

"No," I answered, failing to remember something similar happening before in Laguna and New Orleans, although I didn't pass out then.

"What were you doing when this happened?"

"I was playing ice hockey. I was on the bench. That's the last thing I remember."

"Were you injured?"

"No."

"Did your chest hurt?"

"No."

"Does it hurt now?

"No."

"Any nausea?"

"Nothing. Everything's fine."

He took a couple steps toward the bed and bent over me, looking into each eye with a small flashlight. Taking the stethoscope from his pocket, he put it around his neck and in his ears before moving it across my chest, stopping in a few places.

He put a hand on my shoulder. "We want to check a few things, so relax for a while," he said. "We need to make sure your body is stabilized."

The doctor gave the nurse brief instructions and turned to me.

"I'll be back shortly," he said before vanishing as quickly as he arrived.

The nurse, all business, hooked up an EKG, quickly pasting the small tabs and cables on my chest and legs as if she had done these things a thousand times before. I'm sure she had.

It worried me that they were doing an EKG. Did they suspect passing out was connected to the heart? I asked the nurse.

"It's what the doctor ordered," she said,

That didn't answer my question, which was frustrating.

I wanted to call Pat. The nurse finished, left the room for a moment, and returned.

"Let's take your blood pressure one more time and see how you're doing now," she said, wrapping the sleeve around my arm.

"How is it?"

"A little high, but that's okay. Just relax and I'll be right back."

I lay there with concern.

What was it I had experienced at the rink? I asked myself. *What was that bright light I was being pulled toward? Why? What does it mean? Was it a near-death experience?*

A shiver went up my spine. I closed my eyes.

It must have been another ten minutes before the nurse came back, carrying a small tray with a plastic glass of orange juice.

"I brought you some juice," she said with a slight grin. "This should help you regain some of your energy and strength."

With my throat dry and my stomach empty, the taste was like a jolt of electricity running through my veins. Orange juice never went down so well.

The doctor eventually returned, looking at the clipboard he was carrying. He took a quick glance at me.

"Your tests checked out. Your blood pressure is normal. The EKG was uneventful. The scan was fine." Then, lowering the chart to his side, he asked, "Do you have a family doctor?"

"Yes," I said.

"I recommend you call him in the morning and make an appointment for a thorough examination. It could be nothing, but you did lose consciousness."

I thanked him, and he vanished again. Then I remembered I needed a ride back to the rink, where my car was parked.

It had been a furious few hours and was now near midnight. Apparently one of the players at the rink had driven to the hospital and dropped off my hockey bag, which had my civilian clothes.

I was grateful for everyone's professional care and for the quick action of the paramedics, but I had no idea why I lost consciousness. Nor did anyone at the hospital.

***

The hospital had called Pat when I arrived. She finally got there, bursting into the small room as I was getting dressed. It was good to see her.

Looking stressed, her hair messy, no makeup, wearing old sweats and tennis shoes, she'd been about to go to bed.

We hugged. She spoke rapidly. "Honey, are you okay? What happened? They called me. How are you?"

"I'm okay. Nothing serious. I simply passed out at the rink. Sorry to put you through this."

"If it's not serious," she persisted, "why are you in the hospital?"

She turned to an orderly standing there. "What happened?" He quickly called the nurse who had been with me since I'd arrived.

She came in. "Mrs. Tar?"

"Yes," Pat responded anxiously. "Is my husband alright? What happened?"

The nurse gave Pat a quick summation. "We suggest he see your family doctor for a more thorough examination."

It sounded like one of those recorded statements when you phone your doctor's office and a recorded voice says, "If this is an emergency, call 911. . . ."

Clutching a chart, the nurse went on, "We'll enclose a copy of the test results with his discharge papers. He'll need to sign some papers before being released."

Pat thanked her, and before she could ask anything else, I said, "Let's get out of here. I'll tell you on the way to the rink."

"The rink!" she blurted. "Aren't you coming home?"

"I am, but my car is at the rink."

"Are you okay to drive?"

"I am."

We quickly stopped at the rink.

Driving home with Pat following behind me, I tried to reconstruct the entire evening. Despite being outwardly calm, my chest felt tight. I was worried. No one could explain why or what had happened. My body had been on the player's bench but not me.

A LOSS, A SCARE

One day I received a phone call from my sister Irene. She was out of town and concerned about our brother Les.

"He hasn't answered his phone in several days, and I heard he hasn't been at work either," she said.

Les was very close to her. She had taken him under her wing when he was fifteen after my mother died in Detroit. When Irene moved to California several years later, he did too. I still had two older brothers and two older sisters living in Detroit.

"He wasn't at the rink the other night either," I said. We played hockey together every week. "Maybe he's just under the weather."

I told her I'd call him, and if he didn't answer, I'd go to his apartment.

He didn't answer.

When I got to his apartment, the fire department paramedics were there, and the police were standing at the door talking with a woman, apparently the apartment manager.

I walked toward the open door, and she approached me. Pleasant looking, middle-aged, and tidy, she held up her hand. "May I help you?"

"Yes, I'm Les's brother. He hasn't responded to phone calls. I'm just checking on him."

She looked down for a second, then nodded to the police officer, who stepped aside.

Inside, another police officer was talking to the firefighters. The manager said, "This is his brother." The officer took a step forward and stood directly in front of me. "Your name?"

"Ed. Ed Tar," I said as a flush of fear went down my spine.

"And you are . . . ?"

"Les's brother."

He paused, swallowed, and peered into my eyes. "I'm sorry to have to tell you your brother has passed away."

I was speechless, stunned, and confused. Les had just turned thirty-seven years old. What was he saying? A shiver went up my spine. *This doesn't make sense. He was vigorous and in good health.* I looked beyond the officer, across the room at a fully clothed, shoeless body lying atop an unmade bed in this small, messy studio apartment.

"When did you last see your brother?"

"Just last week," I said, my words stumbling to get out. "We played hockey together." I stood frozen for a moment when I felt the hand of the officer reach for my arm.

"Would you like to sit down?

"No!"

They wanted a positive identification. "Could we ask you to please confirm this is your brother?"

I inched myself toward him lying there. The walls seemed to close in. My eyes began to water. The silence in the room was deafening as the firefighters, police officer, and apartment manager stood watching. I didn't want to acknowledge it was him. He looked different. His face was puffy and bloated like someone with an overdose of Botox.

I choked up and, barely able to talk, finally mumbled, "Yes, that's Les." I reached out my hand to touch him but quickly turned away to take a breath.

Trying to gather myself, I asked the apartment manager, "What happened?"

She didn't know. "I found him there when I entered his apartment at the request of your sister Irene."

Neither the police nor firefighters had any answers either. The coroner had been called. Numb with a deep feeling of loss and my head in a fog, I thought of Irene. I had to call her back to give her the tragic news.

She let out a shriek. "Oh no! Oh my God! No!" I heard her say to someone nearby, "My brother Les died."

"What happened? How? Why? Tell me," Irene cried.

"When I arrived, the police and fire department were already there," I said sadly. "No one had any answers."

I heard the sorrow in her voice. "We're leaving and will be home in a few hours."

It was surreal. I called Pat. She was stunned. "What can I do? Where are you? I'm so sorry."

"I'm at his apartment," I said. "I'll be coming home shortly once they remove his body." The past hour had been surreal.

An autopsy showed he had died from a brain tumor the size of a golf ball. He had complained about nagging headaches but hadn't gone to the doctor to find out what might be causing them.

It was the first death of a sibling in our large family of seven, and it shocked everyone. We took him back home to Detroit for burial. It was strange flying back, knowing his body was in the compartment below where we were sitting.

***

It was difficult getting back to work and especially going to the rink without Les there. We'd shared so many stories together driving back and forth.

A few months later, I decided to give it a try and play hockey in a pickup game. I was nervous, unsettled, and felt alone thinking about Les when the game began.

During the game, that same strange feeling again overtook my body—intense heat, redness, itching, tightness in my throat, trouble breathing. My legs were like lead, my equipment irritating my skin. I remembered what the doctor had told me: "If you are feeling unsettled, immediately get yourself out of the situation you're in."

I turned to Gordy, one of the players on the bench, and told him I was leaving.

He knew of my past experience. "Are you okay?" he asked.

"Yeah. I'm going to call it a night," I said, grabbing my gloves and helmet before going over the boards toward the locker room, about thirty feet from the ice.

I collapsed before getting there. The next thing I recall was lying on the floor with players leaning over me. As I came to, Gordy and another player were supporting my body.

"I was just about to start mouth-to-mouth resuscitation and call the paramedics," Gordy said.

He was a take-control type of guy on and off the ice. He was respected for his play and his levelheadedness.

Gordy worked for a medical supply company and had an innate sense of what to do in emergency situations. I was grateful he was there but embarrassed about what happened—again!

They helped me up to the dressing room. Forty-five minutes later, feeling better but a bit confused and concerned, I left the rink and drove home. A fearful thought swept across my mind: *My father was an epileptic. Is this related? Am I moving in that direction?*

Something was seriously wrong. This was the third time, and there were other times when I'd felt uneasy and simply brushed it off. I never took seriously what a doctor had told me after it had happened before, but I was determined to try again to understand what was going on with me and my health.

The past few years had been extremely stressful with employees to worry about, steady clients who kept us busy, and a TV series.

BE NIMBLE

Many large companies with sprawling dealer networks across North America go through the annual ritual of introducing new products to their dealers before the public sees them. Often these introductions are lavish and costly events in hotel exhibit halls or convention centers.

Every tool available to draw attention to their products is used to create excitement and interest: Hollywood performers; film, video, and special live sketches; pyrotechnics; orchestras; magicians—even animals.

With one particular event I hoped to produce for my client, seven hundred dealers were expected to attend. During my early meetings with them at their corporate offices, I proposed using singers and dancers onstage to help create excitement and bring attention to their products.

"When the curtain opens and the product is revealed," I told them, "an enthusiastic cast will burst onto the stage.

They'll break into specially written musical numbers singing praises of the product and brief sketches calling attention to features and benefits. Everyone has probably seen something similar in big TV commercials. But we'll be live onstage."

The three company executives sat silently in the small, stuffy conference room. I was nervous, sensing they were unsure as they exchanged furtive glances. This was my most important and largest client. The stakes were high. I couldn't let this get away.

I went on. "Our cast will carry the wholesome family image your company prides itself on. The energy will be high and the message clear and strong."

"That's good," muttered one of them as another nodded in agreement. They launched into a series of detailed questions for the next half hour.

When they said, "Okay, let's do it," I wasn't sure who was more excited, them or I.

There are no second takes producing an onstage live show. If there's a mistake, it's out there for everyone to see. It also requires a different creative team than for a film or videotape, including a writer versed in writing for stage productions who understands the reality of a stage environment, what's possible, and what's not. I chose one of my go-tos, Bob, to write it.

My attention turned to the next most important person on the team, a director and, in this case, one who could also weave in choreography.

Alex fit the bill. We'd worked together before. He lived in West Hollywood but retained his New York attitude and blunt mannerisms. In his younger days, he'd danced in a few Broadway shows and, moving west, had added directing to his résumé—especially corporate shows.

Alex was slender, stood maybe five feet ten, walked with a bit of a swagger, had thinning dark hair and a sharpness in his voice that cut through clutter.

"I know exactly who could complement the product," he crowed during lunch in Hollywood as I gave him an overview of what I had in mind.

I didn't like to prejudge talent before seeing them, but Alex was just being boastful Alex.

Once the scripts were approved, we began the process of casting the show.

Not all agents in LA had talent interested in auditioning for corporate shows, but we knew the few who did. They were eager to answer our call and sent us résumés and headshots of experienced union talent. Alex and I picked who we wanted to audition and let the agents know. Most talent in Hollywood wait for their big break in TV or films. While they wait, though, performing in a corporate show is a good way to earn decent money.

For the auditions and rehearsals, I rented one of the halls in the historic Hollywood Masonic Temple on Hollywood's Walk of Fame. The granite-clad structure sat across the street from the legendary Grauman's Chinese Theater, where stars' handprints are imbedded in the sidewalk.

Because of its variety of rooms with thick, soundproof walls; hardwood floors; and airy high ceilings, it was a favorite for many producers. A singer's voice could carry, a dancer had room to maneuver, and the fee was easy on the producer's wallet.

Sitting at the audition table and judging performers was not as easy as it appeared. We—Alex, me, and my musical director, Don—were looking for a triple threat: talent who could sing, dance and act. Don had composed music for

TV, films, concerts, and multiple corporate shows and knew the musical range of talent.

One by one, the performers came in to audition, many carrying a piece of sheet music they wanted to sing. They would hand it to Don or the piano player we had. If they didn't bring their own music, they'd sing what we gave them.

If someone showed up late for their audition, it raised a yellow flag no matter their excuse. If they couldn't be on time for an audition, would they be on time for rehearsals or even the show?

Following one female singer's audition and dance routine, she left the room, and Alex leaned back in his chair, tilted his head up, and said confidently with his distinctive New York bravado, "I've worked with Vicki before. She's terrific. She'll know her lines and can dance and sing up a storm."

A few others had a more challenging time winning us over. After a wonderful singer left the room, I said, "Well, he can really sing."

Alex rolled his eyes. "Yes, but he's somewhat stiff and had difficulty reading the six lines we gave him without stumbling. I'm not sure he'd be good with the product."

Another time he'd comment enthusiastically, "She's a great dancer. What'd you think, Don? How's her voice?"

Frowning, Don looked at Alex and shot a glance at me. "Her singing voice doesn't have the widest range, but with rehearsal, I think I can get her to reach the notes."

Picking talent is intensely collaborative. Since I had worked several times with Alex and Don, we knew each other well and could be candid without causing offense. The room became stuffy as we went back and forth during the day, making notes on the talent's résumés and photos covering the spaces on our table between empty paper coffee cups.

We considered not only the talent's audition that day but also previous shows they'd been in and the agent's knowledge of the person—anything that could shed light on their experience. In my mind I asked, *What are the risks with this person? Do they convey the right image? Will they represent the client in a good way?*

I always invited the client to the audition, but being busy, they simply preferred to look at photos of those we selected.

Late in the afternoon, we reached a consensus on six performers. I notified their agents.

With the scripts complete and a cast selected, we began ten days of rehearsals.

During the same time, I was meeting with my film crew and editors, finalizing the film segments and various visuals we'd use in the show. Richard, my set designer, was talking with a local source in Louisville, site of the show, for the necessary set pieces and drapes. I also opted to rent the bulk of technical equipment, lights, screens, and sound in Louisville to keep costs down rather than bring them from LA. Even keeping an eye on the tiniest details, however, there's the possibility of the unexpected.

Dialogue in the show would be live, but because of the volume of choreography and movement onstage, we decided to prerecord the cast musical numbers in a Hollywood recording studio. Onstage, they'd lip-synch, singing softly to their voices. This wasn't unusual when large musical dance numbers were involved. The music tracks were on audiotape at the time. Today, the tracks are all safely digital.

The sixty-foot stage had been set up over the previous three days in the convention center, and the dress rehearsals the day before the show went well.

A worrier, I went to bed that night with my mind going over details, reminding myself, *We've dotted every I and crossed every T.*

Or so I thought.

***

The morning of the show, there was the usual frenzy of activity backstage, with the cast in makeup and getting dressed. The crew was in its final technical checks. Even though I had been through this many times in my career, the anxious feeling of staging a show never goes away. Seven hundred dealers were finishing breakfast in an adjacent hall. Doors were to open at 9 a.m.

A few minutes before nine, as I always did prior to a show, I walked to the control booth to give them thumbs-up to "run the music" for opening doors.

There was commotion in the booth. Gathered around the soundboard and tape machines that held the music tracks for the show, Alex, Don, the stage manager, and the sound tech were deep in an animated discussion.

Usually at this time, the booth was calm, waiting for my cue:

"What's going on?" I asked.

"We have a problem," Alex said, trying to remain calm. "The main tape deck just died."

"Switch to the backup," I said intuitively. "We have a crowd of people at the door."

"Hold the doors," Alex demanded, New York anger rising in his voice.

"They brought the wrong backup tape deck. It's useless," he said.

My heart about stopped. *Didn't someone check on that before? What the hell's wrong with them? Without the music tracks, we don't have a show.*

A thousand thoughts raced through my mind. *Are there any numbers or sketches the performers could perform without the music tracks? Should we just go with the executive presentations alone? Would the audience even know there were supposed to be musical numbers? Do we say anything onstage? Why did I hire this local sound company in the first place? We could have brought everything from LA.*

The client, Jim, had been standing near the doors and was now walking toward me. "Ed, when are you opening the doors? People are ready to come in."

"Yes, I know," I said. "We're having a small problem with one of the tape decks. We need to hold the doors for a few moments."

The tension in the empty hall was enormous. By then, the talent and the entire crew knew what was going on.

Jim glanced at the furious activity in the booth, then back at me. With audible stress, he asked, "How long will it be?"

"Ten, maybe fifteen minutes," I said, feeling tension throughout my body. "They're bringing a backup deck from backstage. It'll be patched into the soundboard and tested."

I didn't want to tell him the risk of doing that would mean there would be no crucial backup deck backstage triggering projectors either. I could feel my chest tighten and a slight pulse in my temples as the pressure mounted.

The sound tech was finally lifting the replacement into position, feverishly patching in cables.

At that moment, David, a young client staffer, walked up. "Dealers are ready to come in," he said.

"It's going to be a few minutes!" Jim told him, sounding irritated. "We'll let you know!"

David gave a darting glance at the control booth, hesitated, then turned and walked back toward the doors.

It was nearly 9:20 a.m. The doors remained closed.

Then I heard Alex holler, "We got it! We're testing it!"

Everyone stopped and held their breath. The tech pushed the button, the light lit, the tapes began spinning, and we were in business. We had no backup. It had to work.

I said, "Okay, run the music." The doors were opened. For the next hour, I paced in the back of the room with moist palms, crossed fingers, and a prayer on my lips as the cast performed beautifully.

The show was a huge success.

As the room emptied, I walked to the control booth to express my gratitude, smiling and filled with relief. Alex stood there with Don, the stage manager, the audio tech, and others. He looked at me, rolled his shoulders, held out his arms, and took a beat.

"What?" he said with a slight grin. "I never doubted it'd work."

We all burst out laughing, releasing some of the tension, knowing how close we had come to a disaster.

"I'm going backstage to thank the cast," I said.

"Hold on, I'll go with you." Alex stepped down from the booth.

He put his hand on my shoulder as we walked together toward the stage.

"That was a close one," he said.

***

Some clients were open to having well-known celebrities or athletes talk or perform at their event, such as Lou Holtz, Joe Theismann, Jonathan Winters, the Smothers Brothers, or any number of celebrities and entertainment acts popular at the time. Who wouldn't want the attention and excitement a celebrity brings? But ultimately, money talked: tight budgets played a part in who we had.

A couple producer friends said working with name talent puts you in the path of big egos and high demands. On the contrary, I found them easy to work with. They were always on time, friendly, eager to please, and complimentary in their act about the client and the products. I avoided performers who had several pages of demands attached to their contract.

In many shows, introducing a key executive in an unusual, creative way always raised an eyebrow. A few high-level executives didn't see the point, while others were happy to try something more fun and unique than simply walking onstage.

Ed, the vice president of sales and marketing of a large publicly traded company, always wanted to be different. He was a jovial guy who was open to trying just about anything. When I presented the idea of his riding out onstage on the back of a 1600-pound longhorn steer in San

Antonio, he was excited to do it. When he saw the size of the steer backstage, however, he looked concerned.

"It's time to mount up," I told him.

A cowboy wrangler held the rope attached to the steer as he got on. There was no saddle. Longhorns are known to be docile, but for some reason, this one wasn't happy. Irritated, it started to twist and shift around as the wrangler pulled tighter on the rope.

The show announcer introduced him. As the curtain opened, western music played, and a spotlight illuminated them as they came out onstage, nudged by the wrangler. Ed, a big man of some 230 pounds, waved to the audience. Reaching center stage, he was supposed to dismount. Somehow his foot got tangled in the rope that was wrapped around the steer. The steer, now angry, was shifting from side to side. His hind legs came up. The audience reacted with a "whoa!" and a laugh. Standing in the back of the room, I knew something was wrong, and my heart sank. The steer's legs came up again as he twisted toward the audience. Another wrangler came onstage to help calm him. Ed slipped sideways, his foot still tangled in the rope, until he broke free and slid off into one of the wrangler's arms. The other one pulled the upset steer away. The audience began to sense it hadn't been planned that way. What happened if someone was injured was always on my mind when we tried something a bit different.

Ed took a step away from the steer. Everything captured on the thirty-foot screens positioned next to the stage. Ever the salesman, he smiled, regained his composure, waved to the audience, and patted the steer as the two handlers led it offstage.

"I never rode a steer before," he said. "Not sure I want to ride this one again."

The audience erupted in laughter and applause.

Another time, in Las Vegas, to introduce him, with music and dramatic effects, we flew the same executive twenty feet in the air from back stage, over the entire set and landed him on stage where two La Vegas show girls came out to remove his harness.

Working with celebrities and bringing something unusual to a corporate show was fun, but my fear was always the same: Will it work? Will this cost me a client if it doesn't? It never did.

***

Most of the corporate shows took me out of town for several days at a time. When in town, I tried to make it a point to be at home for dinner every night with Pat and the kids. It was extremely important we sit down and plan our lives together as a family.

With a ten-year age difference between Heather and Donovan, conversations around the table always included a wide range of interests. When Heather was deciding on colleges to attend, Donovan was simply enjoying being a kid of eight years old hoping to get his first pair of rollerblades.

A TRIM AND A PIANO

Stars, celebrities, the rich and powerful—all tend to require tender loving care to maintain their starlike qualities, not to mention their egos. Like many, I've watched them parade their privilege and carefully manicured self-image before the public. Naturally, Hollywood is chock-full of people standing ready to provide whatever "update" (whether a facelift, coiffed hair, stunning pearl white teeth, or a new toned body) that such people desire.

One day, while Pat and I were dressing to go to dinner, I took a look in the mirror and casually remarked, "I need to find a new barber. I don't like my hair."

She shot a quick glance at me.

As I tried to carefully comb it, my patience ran out. I threw the comb down.

"Damnit, my hair looks terrible," I said, studying it in the mirror. "My barber doesn't say much other than 'wash it more.' He's only interested in getting to the next guy sitting there."

Hoping she might say I was too sensitive, that no, my hair looked fine, Pat stopped what she was doing, took another look, and said, "It *does* look terrible and uneven. Find a new barber!"

She has a way of not wasting words. My confidence took a hit.

"I have no idea where to look," I said with another wince at the mirror.

"You'll find someone. Let's go, or we'll be late." She walked out of the bedroom, hitting the light switch to turn the lights off so I wouldn't linger. That felt strange. I'm usually the one trying to hurry her along.

We went out for the evening and forgot about hair.

A few days later, Pat came home from an audition at one of the studios. We sat down for dinner with the kids, Heather and Donovan, exchanging details about our day.

Pat said, "I talked with someone today who had great hair."

She paused, waiting for my reaction.

"Uh-ha?" I muttered, reaching across the table for the salad.

"I asked him where he gets it cut because you were looking for a new barber."

She'd never been shy about talking to people, asking anything that came into her active mind.

"What? You asked a guy where he gets his hair cut?'

"Sure," she said, passing me the bowl. "I wanted to know, and he was flattered."

I chuckled. "Only you would do that."

"He told me he has it cut in Hollywood," she said, "by a barber they call Little Joe. He cuts the hair of many Hollywood celebrities and is supposed to be very good." She took a breath. "If you're interested, you'll have to call information for his phone number because he didn't have it."

I took a sip of water and cleared my throat. "Do you think the operator is going to have the phone number of some barber in Hollywood named Little Joe?" *This is going to be fruitless*, I thought.

"It's up to you," she said casually. "There's nothing wrong with asking."

Heather and Donovan were seemingly uninterested in what we were talking about until Heather chimed in. "You could use a haircut, Dad."

Donovan simply added, "Yeah."

I looked at them. "Thanks a lot."

Kids are always very direct with their comments.

Still skeptical, I dialed zero for the operator later that evening (remember, this was well before googling!). She was very helpful, and in a few moments, we'd narrowed the name down to a couple of barber possibilities. The next morning, a bit anxious, I called both numbers, and as luck would have it, one of them was the Little Joe Pat had described. His hair salon was on Hollywood Boulevard, near Beverly Hills.

I didn't rank as one of the Hollywood elites, but in the back of my mind, I kept thinking, *I deserve a good haircut from someone who knows what they're doing. I've been to enough average barbers who simply sit you down, chop up your hair, and send you off.* I wanted more than that. Most of the top corporate executives I called on were well groomed. They obviously took pride in their appearance. It was important for me to do the same if I was hoping to land their work. It's amazing how even small things, like a haircut, can pay off with huge professional dividends.

The receptionist on the other end of the line was friendly as we set an appointment two weeks later. Little Joe was busy. I dared ask what he charged and tried to act nonchalant when she told me. I thought, *I could get ten haircuts for that price, but hey, this is my treat.*

I quickly called Pat. "I'm so happy," she said, sounding excited. "You'll like him."

"How do you know?" I responded. "You don't know anything about him."

"If he cuts the hair of the rich and famous, he's good," she said.

Little Joe was in fact the stylist and barber to many of Hollywood's top superstars and producers. Names such as Robert Wagner, Norman Lear, Martin Sheen. Marlon Brando, Jimmy Stewart, and a wide host of others had been in his chair. Some of the Rat Pack even summoned him to Las Vegas to do a cut before their shows. He'd been close friends with Bruce Lee, long before Lee became well known. Joe also cut his hair.

When the time came, my first thought when stepping into Joe's upscale, swank, and elegant salon was *This is not your average barber.* There was no candy cane barber pole anywhere to be seen. The ambience in the reception area, with its oak walls, live green plants, soft music, and the smell of leather hanging in the air, was classic rich.

At the reception desk, a beautiful, smiling young lady greeted me. "Good morning. Mr. Tar?"

"Yes."

"Welcome. Please have a seat. I'll let Joe know you're here."

I took a seat on the plush leather sofa. Next to it were two small end tables that held the latest copies of the *Hollywood Reporter* and *Variety* magazine, daily bibles for people in "the biz." A few framed and autographed photos of Hollywood stars hung tastefully on the walls.

In a moment, Joe came out. He was slight in stature with thick dark hair, high cheekbones, steady dark eyes, and a friendly smile. His voice was calm.

"Hi, Ed," he said, extending his hand. "I'm Joe Torrenueva. Welcome. Please come in."

We walked a few feet down a hall to his private room, where he performed his magic. The wall facing the corridor was frosted glass like the door. With a flip of a switch, the glass turned opaque for privacy. It only added to that "special" feeling his salon conveyed for the rich and famous . . . and me!

It was a large room that could easily hold two or three chairs but held just one—his. More personally autographed photos hung on the wall. A photo of his wife and children sat on the counter below the mirror.

I took off my jacket to hang, and he quickly said, "Please, I'll take care of that for you." He carefully put it on a padded coat hanger before he hung it.

I think I'm going to like it here.

Turns out, he'd learned his special hairstyling skills as the protégé of famed international celebrity hairstylist Jay Sebring in Hollywood in the late sixties.

Before charging in as some barbers always do, he carefully explored my hair, running his fingers through it as if panning for gold, holding up strands on the top, sides, and back.

"Your hair is very dry," he said, watching my reaction in the mirror. "But I'll take care of that. When it's cut, it'll be more balanced and healthier looking."

We talked about the style. He asked if I'd scheduled a manicure.

"No, I'm fine." This was definitely a new experience for me.

Joe cared about what he was doing, and there was no rushing. Before the cut, I settled in for a shampoo. He draped the cloth over my shoulders and around my neck.

I sat back in the chair as he lowered my head under the warm water. His hands vigorously worked the shampoo and conditioner through my hair. My scalp tingled. He rinsed it and placed a towel on my head to remove the loose water as I sat up.

He took care examining the hair again before his scissors and comb went to work, shaping my new haircut.

I could understand why celebrities liked him; his reassuring demeanor, quiet voice, and confident hands made me feel important. He was a sculptor in his private room. I knew I was in the right place. We engaged in conversation. He wanted to know about my work.

Joe mentioned a few of the people who'd sat in that same chair. He was very careful and didn't say anything about them we probably didn't know already, though I could imagine he'd heard many a story. His voice conveyed how proud he was of his work, his reputation, and his long powerful client list. Through his connections, he'd also managed to raise large sums of money for various charities and schools.

It was an hour before he finished. He took a step back and very gently put his fingers on my temples.

"How do you like it?" he asked, looking in the mirror with pride.

"It looks great! It looks thicker."

He smiled. "It's actually not." He pointed to the top and side. "I cut it shorter. It gives the illusion of fuller hair when cut correctly." He quickly added, "It'll grow out looking good as well."

I didn't question him.

He removed the apron. I stood up, and he brushed my clothes with a soft brush, removing any loose hair. I didn't get that in my neighborhood barbershop. He reached for my jacket and held it as I put it on.

"Thank you very much for coming in," he said. "I hope you enjoy your haircut."

"I will," I told him as we walked to the lobby. Smiling at the receptionist, I handed her a check. As I was leaving, Martin Sheen, Joe's close friend, entered.

"Martin, nice to see you again," Joe said.

That evening at dinner, Pat was anxious to hear about my experience.

"I like him!" I told her.

"Good. I had a feeling you would." We hugged. "Turn around. Let me see how it looks." As I quickly spun around, she said, "Looks great!"

I've been going to Joe ever since.

***

On more than one occasion, Pat brought up the subject of encouraging Donovan to play a musical instrument. He was eight years old at the time,

"If he took up an instrument," she said rather cheekily, "he might even play in one of your corporate shows someday."

"He'd really like to play hockey," I said. "He asked more than once when we were at the last Kings game."

Pat stared at me.

"And he asked again when I took him public skating a few weeks ago. They have a youth hockey program at the ice rink."

She broke eye contact with a frustrating shake of her head. We were in the bedroom getting ready for bed. "Would there be time for him to play an instrument?"

I didn't answer.

"Hockey is only a couple hours on the weekend, right?" she asked, looking at me for an answer with expectant raised eyebrows.

"Yes," I said. "Saturday mornings."

"Okay. Good." She took a step closer with a quick kiss on the cheek as if to say, *That's fine! He'll play an instrument.*

Having taken guitar lessons for a short time as a young kid, I knew the satisfaction of being able to actually play an instrument. However, Donovan was not keen on the idea. Yet after some nudging, he settled on the piano.

Purchasing a piano took some careful shopping. We held off on buying one until we were sure he would continue with it. Pianos were expensive. We ended up with an upright that fit our budget and space in our home.

Pat enrolled him in Yamaha piano lessons. Even with her busy career, she managed to find the time to drive him to class every week, though he complained repeatedly on the way. "Why do I have to go to piano lessons after school when my friends are outside playing?"

He resisted practice but managed to do whatever it took to remain in the class of young pianists.

"I want to play rock and roll," he said, "not those boring recital pieces they teach us."

Despite his resistance, he soon picked up a good ear and began playing by ear. That didn't sit well with the piano teacher in class or at home with the private teacher we brought in.

"If he wants to be good player," they insisted, "he has to read music."

One night, I arrived home from work and was greeted by Pat's big smile. I heard Donovan at the living room piano.

Walking toward him, I noticed a handwritten piece of music on the piano.

"Hi, Donovan. That sounds good. What are you playing?"

He stopped and casually said, "Oh, it's just a song I wrote."

"What? You wrote a song?"

Pat jumped in enthusiastically. "Doesn't it sound great?"

"Oh, Mom," Donovan said, shrugging. "It's not done yet."

"Still, I think it's terrific," she said. "You *are* very talented."

His teachers agreed. He performed in class recitals at the school with the other students, playing classical pieces. Like the few nervous parents sitting in the audience, Pat and I included, we thought whatever he played was good, warts and all.

The teacher at Yamaha eventually arranged for his class to perform before a much larger audience, in Loyola Marymount University's Murphy Recital Hall, a 212-seat space with warm tones of fixed wooden acoustical panels, enough for some to dub it an "acoustical gem." It was nearly full, packed with college students, university music instructors, some faculty, and, of course, nervous parents and grandparents.

Pat was honored when, because of her show biz experience, the piano teacher asked if she would be the onstage MC. She accepted.

During the recital, groups of three or four students played various classical numbers they had been learning in class. In addition, each student had the option to pick a piece of their choice to perform solo. Most picked a somewhat nondescript piece. Not Donovan. After several classical numbers by other students, it was his turn.

Pat, the MC, announced, "Now, ladies and gentlemen, for something a bit different, Donovan Tar will be playing and singing the classic rock and roll piece 'Great Balls of Fire' by Jerry Lee Lewis."

Some in the audience must have been surprised. Dressed in an all-white suit, white shirt, and white tie and with his long blond hair flowing, Donovan walked across the stage to the grand piano. He sat on the bench and paused. There was dead silence in the hall. I sat in the audience, my hands clasped tightly.

The silence was soon broken as his fingers struck the piano keys and his voice sang out. His singing was loud, clear, and energetic. His hands flew rapidly over the keys.

When the last note rang out, there was silence again. It lasted maybe three or four seconds but to me felt like thirty or forty.

Then the audience erupted in applause, even a few cheers. Donovan stood up, walked to center stage, bowed, and calmly walked off. His performance added needed energy to a long, rather dull recital.

Pat and I were very proud of him for sticking to what he wanted to do and, being only nine, going against the norm. He'd bet on himself and won!

UP A WALL

It's often difficult to separate work goals from personal ones.

One Sunday morning, I read an article in the newspaper about a rock climbing school that triggered a rather bizarre thought: *That might be fun to try.*

The article talked about some of the challenges, and at one point said, "It definitely takes you away from your everyday routine."

My long days at work had been brutal lately, balancing potential new clients while taking care of existing ones. I needed to break the routine to keep me fresh. I'd been practicing tai chi for two years, taught by a Chinese master. It helped me a great deal, but I needed a new challenge.

I set the newspaper aside and thought, *I bet I could rock climb.* I'd seen climbers on TV and admired their skill, risk-taking, and independence. Unable to completely erase the thought, a few days later, I dug out that paper and decided to trace down the school. I called and talked with the owner, Rick.

He held classes and trained climbers in Idyllwild, in the San Jacinto Mountains above Palm Springs. As I listened to him talk, my excitement grew. Questioning my sanity in wanting to hang by my fingertips on the side of a rock—but nevertheless persuaded by his enthusiasm—I signed up. I hoped to convince a couple friends to join me, but there were no takers.

Pat had no interest in rock climbing and didn't even know what it was. When I told her about my plan to try it, her first question was "Why?," followed by "Is it safe?"

I quickly assured her it was. "I'll be fine," I said, trying to calm her concern. "The trainer is very experienced. Don't worry."

I detected anxiety as she crossed her arms. I reached out and gently took her hand, pulled her closer to me, and gave her a soft kiss.

"You be careful," she said, her green eyes wide and bright.

For the next month, my imagination went into overdrive, and my vocabulary expanded with words such as *chalk bag* (which holds the chalk to dip your hands in to absorb perspiration and improve your grip), *bucket* (the helmet we'd wear), *belayer* (the person on the ground who manages the rope tied to us), and *body harness* (which is worn around the waist with leg loops where the climbing rope is attached). Then there were *anchors*, *rock ratings*, *carabiners*, *pitch*, *pitons*—the list goes on.

Idyllwild sits about five thousand feet in altitude and is considered one of the top rock-climbing areas in the US. It gained notoriety among climbers with rocks named

Tahquitz (also known as Lily) and Suicide. I was excited setting off on the three-hour drive from LA to Idyllwild.

The road narrowed as it wound up the mountain through tall pines to the village. Arriving, I checked into the small, rustic log-cabin-style motel where our group of six climbers and Bob were staying. He had scheduled an orientation in the hotel that evening before our first climb the next morning. I was anxious to meet him. He was about five feet nine inches tall. His fingers were long, hands weathered, and his arms and legs looked strong and powerful. His appearance seemed right for someone who'd hung off the side of a rock many times.

The group of climbers were all much younger than me. I was in my early forties. Two of them had some climbing experience. I started to worry. *Did I make the right decision? These guys are going to make me look like a rookie . . .* which I was.

Rick said, "When on the face, it doesn't matter what anyone else has done. Concentrate on your own situation. How are you feeling at that moment on the rock? What's your next move and the one after that?"

That failed to quell my concern.

Exhausted and a bit overwhelmed, I lay in bed later that evening, staring at the cabin ceiling and questioning my decision. *Did I make a mistake? Can I change my mind? What happens if I'm injured? How would that affect Pat and the kids? And my job?*

***

The alarm went off at six the next morning. I forgot the doubts and bounced out of bed, eager to get started.

After breakfast, we began our hike on the uneven winding trail up to Tahquitz Rock. For some reason, I'd envisioned the rock we'd climb would be just a stone's throw from the motel. It wasn't. Cool mountain pine air greeted us as we walked for forty-five minutes. The trail was splendid, a woodland masterpiece.

It was difficult to see Tahquitz initially, which only added to the anticipation. How difficult could climbing be with names like White Maiden's Walkway, which was listed as one of the easiest pitches on Tahquitz with a 5.3 rating? Rock climbing technical ratings go up to 5.11 and higher, with each tenth of a point a major uptick in difficulty.

Arriving, we got our first view of the mammoth Tahquitz, and my pulse started racing. It looked intimidating, with multiple pitches going up.

I blurted out to Rick, "Where will we be climbing?"

Casually pointing to the face that went up at what looked to me like at least an eighty-degree angle, he said, "We begin our climb right over there."

Startled and thinking he might be kidding, I said, "We're going to climb *that*?"

"Yep. There are handholds, crevices, and embedded anchors all the way up!"

Feeling a sense of disbelief, I looked at the climber next to me. He stared back with wide eyes that reflected possibly the same reaction. Under his breath, he asked, "Do you see any of those holds?"

"No," I said quietly.

"Me neither."

The other climbers had a similar reaction, exchanging comments and glances back and forth.

In some places, Tahquitz Rock went up some several hundred feet, though the pitch we'd climb wasn't that high.

"Okay!" Rick called. "Straighten out your gear and get ready to climb. I'll go up and attach the rope."

He dipped his hands into the bag of chalk on his belt, grabbed the rope, and with ease began climbing up about a hundred feet to run the rope through the anchors.

Back on the ground, he gathered us together for some final instructions. "Remember everything we talked about last night. Safety is most important. We'll be 'top roping.'"

The basic process is as follows: A rope runs through a fixed anchor at the top of the climb and back to the belayer on the ground. Climbers are hooked onto the rope with their harness.

"Let's get started," he said, scanning our small group before calling my name. To me it was almost like him saying, "run the music."

I was startled. A flush of adrenaline and fear flowed through my body. I'd hoped someone else would go first so I could see how they did it.

He helped tie the rope onto my harness that wrapped around my waist under the groin and around my upper legs. He checked the knots and carabiners, making sure they were attached correctly.

"Check your chalk bag," he said, sounding like a drill sergeant.

It hung on my belt. I adjusted it to be within easy reach.

The other climbers were quiet, and I felt a bit of panic, wanting to flee. *I'll never be able to do this.*

Maybe sensing my concern, Rick said, "The rope will help prevent you from falling all the way down if you slip."

I froze for a second. "Fall?" *This is real.* My belayer stood on the ground, holding the rope attached to the belayer device. His job was to manage the rope, letting out more as I climbed, holding the rope and bracing to slow a fall or slip.

Every nerve in my body was alive. My heart was pounding.

"Look for the toeholds you'll be standing on," Rick said. "See that one to the right and further up to the left? That's what you're aiming for initially." He pointed to what I thought looked too small to hold. "Notice the handhold near the center."

My mouth was dry. I tried to swallow. Squinting to see the holds, I muttered, "Those are small holds."

"They're good sized. Let's go." His hand was on my back as I took a small step forward.

There's a standard routine when starting a climb in verbally communicating with the belayer.

I said, "On belay."

"Belay on," the belayer responded.

"Climbing," I continued.

"Climb on."

The small nipples, cracks, and holds on the rock came into focus.

"Push up with your legs!" Rick shouted. "They do all the work. Don't pull up by your fingertips. Use your fingers for balance."

I was full of doubt and made the first couple holds, then slipped about six feet back to the ground.

Embarrassed and already breathing heavy, I said to Rick, "I don't think I can do this."

His steady eyes caught mine. "Yes you can," he said, giving me a slap on the back. "Try again."

The newspaper article I had read didn't make rock climbing sound this difficult.

He rattled off words of advice. "Keep your butt tucked in and your back straight. Stay close to the rock. Set your feet before moving your hands."

The other climbers stood there, attuned to what he was saying as it would be their turn soon.

Taking a deep breath, I heard in my mind, *Run the music.*

And so I took a step up, reaching for nipples and crevices on the rock, and soon found myself standing maybe about ten feet off the ground. My arms and legs were shaking. My fingers hurt. I tried to remain focused on the next move. Slowly I moved up, watching for footholds, not wanting them to be too far away from each other.

When you're up forty to fifty feet on the side of a relatively smooth rock with only a rope that you *pray* will hold should you slip, there's no time to think about anything but your next move. Hanging on is physically and mentally demanding, testing your strength, agility, balance, endurance, and guts.

I took another breath. My forearms burned; my legs stiffened. Even my fingernails hurt as the sweat began to pour off my body.

I dipped my hands into the chalk bag to keep them dry and engaged in positive self-talk. *Okay, you can do this. There's a fingerhold up to your right. Reach for it. Watch your foot placement. Push up. There's another hold to your left. Don't look down.*

"It's very important to look two or three steps ahead to where your feet and hands will be," Rick had emphasized during the prior night's orientation. "A wrong move could put you out of position for the next move."

In some respects, all these techniques are similar to business. *Hold on. Scour the terrain for multiple moves forward. Chart your course. Know what you're going to do before doing it. Keep your balance and push on. How many times have I done that, betting on myself to make it work?*

I reached the top and sank to the ground elated, exhausted, and feeling a rush of accomplishment. Other climbers were coming up behind me.

We made other climbs that day as the sun turned hotter and the rock warmed.

One climb particularly claustrophobic for me and others in our group was lying prone on our backs and edging up a crevice cut into the side of the wall. The crevice was only about thirty feet long, twenty-four inches deep, and eighteen inches high, six inches from my face. We had to wiggle our way up on our butt but not too much wiggle or we'd fall off the edge to the ground thirty feet below. I was terrified, feeling trapped, with no option other than to continue.

My body trembled as Rick hollered from below, "Keep moving inch by inch! You're almost there!"

I couldn't bend my legs enough to get much traction. All but one in our group made that prone position climb.

The sun began ebbing behind the rock after that climb. Bob was concerned about possible dampness on the pitches and decided to call it a day. As we walked back to our motel, there was a sense of camaraderie as we exchanged our feelings and thoughts with each other about what we'd experienced. My confidence surged, and there was a lightness in my chest.

The next day, working in teams of two, we worked on our techniques, rappelling off the side of a cliff. It took a couple of attempts under Rick's close instructions and supervision before I felt I knew the basics of how to safely rappel.

***

Returning from Idyllwild, exhausted, I walked into the house Sunday evening, dropped my backpack, and went into Pat's studio. She was at her easel working on a painting. "Hi, honey," I said softly, not wanting to disturb her.

"Hey, how's my rock climber? How was it?" she asked, wiping her forehead with the back of her hand, holding a paintbrush in the other.

I gave her a soft kiss. "It was tough, but it was great!" I answered with a smile. "I did all the climbs. Rappelling off the side of a wall was somewhat nerve-racking until I got the hang of it."

"Hang of it?" She laughed.

We spent several minutes talking about my adventure before I asked, "What're you working on?"

"A Chinese brush painting. It's my first. I'm learning new techniques in the class I'm taking. This one and another are going to be exhibited in a show at the Chinese Cultural Center next month."

"What do you think?" she asked, stepping back, cocking her head and looking at the easel.

"It looks good."

"Good? Is that all?"

"No. . . . I mean. . . . it's incomplete, right? It's colorful. . . ."

"I'm actually going to do three paintings. I'll be busy."

"Sounds good. If I can help with anything, I'm here."

She finished painting for the night and began cleaning her brushes while I unpacked my backpack. We talked the rest of the evening about her art and my recent adventure up a wall.

The following month, I went with her to deliver the paintings to the cultural center. It was always exciting to see her work hung with other creative artists'.

At the show's conclusion, she was honored with an award for creative excellence. She was thrilled. "Not bad for a first-time foray into this type of painting," she said. Most of her paintings up to then had been in acrylic or oil.

***

Several months later, another challenge came before me.

Two of my hockey buddies, while getting dressed in the locker room after a game, said they were going to try once again to make the trek up Mount Whitney in the Sierra Nevada mountains, about two hundred miles north of LA. At 14,500 feet high, it's the highest mountain in the contiguous forty-eight.

"Want to go up Whitney?" Bill asked, his eyes bright and the lines on his face framing his smile. Nearly fifty, he was the oldest guy in the room. He was talkative and friendly and had climbed Whitney several times.

"Ed, all three of us could go again," another player, Dick, chimed in.

We had tried to make the trek before, but less than an hour into it, we were forced to turn back. Torrential rains had washed out the trail and turned small streams into raging rivers four feet deep, while falling rocks added more safety hazards.

A tinge of excitement rose in me. Zipping up my hockey bag and ready to leave, my words stumbled out. "Ah . . . maybe . . . my job . . . my job keeps me pretty busy six days a week. Let me think about it," I said, "and see what's going on at home and at work. Will let you know."

My insides began to turn. The specter of a challenge to go back to Whitney and succeed this time filled my mind. How would Pat respond?

When I arrived home, she was finishing up in her studio. I walked in excited and didn't hesitate to begin telling her what we were thinking of doing. She looked surprised.

"Last time you tried this, it was so dangerous, you were forced to turn around." Her eyes widened. "You could have been seriously injured, and now you want to go again?"

"Last year it was just because of a storm," I said, trying to reassure her. "It'll be better this year."

"Says who?" she retorted with an incredulous look on her face and her arms crossed. "You have two kids at home."

"It's going to be fine," I said, reaching out to touch her arm. She pulled away, responding with an acerbic tone.

"Oh, just like that. Everything's going to be fine. How can you say that? I do worry when my husband is going to climb some mountain and could possibly get injured . . . or worse."

We continued talking about it when she sarcastically remarked, "It's your decision, but that's how I feel." She walked out of the room.

I stood there troubled by her reaction, hoping she'd eventually come around to see my side.

Two weeks later, I saw Bill and told him, "Unless something comes up, I can make it."

As the weeks passed and the day for the climb grew near, my excitement increased. I dug out and double-checked my gear from last year that had sat untouched, spreading everything out to do a quick inventory. My hiking boots still fit. The backpack, sleeping bag, ground cloth, and cooking utensils were in good shape. Dick had the tent he and I would share. All that remained were new water bottles, food, and clothes.

Finally, in early September, we were standing at the starting point, Whitney Portal, elevation 8,300 feet. We'd be trekking to 14,505 feet along an eleven-mile trail to the summit. The weather was cool, a light drizzle filled the air, and my pulse was beating fast as we pulled our backpacks from the car in the parking lot. Other nearby hikers did the same thing.

We quickly slung the packs onto our backs and tightened the straps. My pack felt heavy. We grabbed our water bottles, hats, sunglasses, and walking sticks. We were off. I shared a wide grin with Bill and Dick. Bill knew how to bypass the ranger checking permits. We didn't have one.

Nearly an hour into our climb, Bill remarked, "Remember, guys, this is where we were forced to turn around last year." Feeling confident we wouldn't have to this time, I felt utterly present in the moment, walking in awe of the tall pines standing like beautiful guards, watching over us as we slowly made our way up the demanding uneven trail. The incline changed from gradual to a fairly steep trek on the edge of deep cliffs. I was feeling the weight of the backpack, and my legs also felt heavy. It was breathtaking peering across a view of majestic canyons and towering walls of granite. I'd never been in high mountains like this and thought about Pat. She would have been as awestruck as I was surrounded by this dramatic natural beauty. At about 10,500 feet, Mirror Lake reflected the soaring peaks surrounding us, the wildflower-studded meadows, and the cerulean sky. The light drizzle had stopped long ago, leaving a searing sun to dry our skin and parch our throats. I reached for my water bottle as sweat poured from my body.

Above the tree line at about 11,000 feet, Dick and I began experiencing the effects of the high altitude.

"Have a cracker and some water," Bill said. "It helps with nausea."

The trail became more uneven and severe. Maybe it was from exhaustion, not paying attention, or simply the rocks we were maneuvering over, but I slowed down as my footing became unsteady.

When we were above 12,000 feet, Bill announced, "We'll stop here for the night at trail camp and get acclimated before hitting the summit tomorrow."

Those were welcome words. We'd been on the trail for nearly eight hours. I dropped the pack off my back and sat down. In a moment, I was lying prone on the ground, my eyes closed, feeling completely drained and wanting to sleep. My shoulders and lower back ached. My legs tingled. It felt good to stretch out. Dick was full of energy and began setting up our tent. He was feeling much better than he had been a couple hours ago when we thought he was becoming hypothermic after getting wet and the temperature dropping suddenly. Bill and I took turns wrapping him in our arms to transfer some of our body heat to him.

Now setting up camp, Bill began giving more annoying instructions. I just wanted to rest.

"Make sure your tent is on high ground so if it rains tonight, you won't be flooded. Hang your food. There's a community latrine about seventy-five yards away, over there." He pointed to a space surrounded by tarps. A few other hikers dotted the area in the distance.

***

After a restless night in sleeping bags, we were up early; made a cup of hot chocolate; grabbed a Clif Bar, water, and our day pack; and began the hike up an unrelenting set of ninety-six switchbacks toward the summit of Mount Whitney.

It was slow, strenuous, and intense.

My legs were on fire, my head throbbed with each step, and nausea never left me. Sucking in thinning air, defiantly brushing aside thoughts about stopping, I pressed on.

Light snow began to fall at about 14,000 feet. It was refreshing. The switchbacks turned slick and treacherous.

Drawing close to the summit, I gained a second wind when we saw a small stone hut about the size of a two-car garage. Bill's eyes widened. There was excitement in his voice when he said, "That's where we'll go in to sign the visitor book."

"Visitor book?" I repeated blankly. "You're kidding."

My adrenaline rushed as we approached the hut. Then I saw the sign: *Mount Whitney, Elevation, 14,505 feet*. My heart beat against my chest. We'd reached the top!

The hut, built for astronomers in 1909 by the Smithsonian, had been put on the National Register of Historic Places in 1977. The visitor book sat on a table inside. We smiled as we each signed it.

Walking outside the hut to take in the unobstructed panoramic view, I held my arms high above my head, excitement filling my body. Feeling awake with an adrenaline rush, my eyes took in every rugged peak below us. With a slow, disbelieving shake of my head, I gazed out at the grandeur of the high Sierra Nevada mountain range. We were above the entire lower forty-eight states. My mouth fell open in wonder as my mind raced. *Am I really on top of a mountain?*

It seemed only about twenty minutes before the weather took another sudden turn and the snow began falling harder.

"We need to start going down," Bill insisted.

The switchbacks were wet and slippery. Fortunately, we weren't wearing our heavy backpacks as we made our way down to trail camp. Exhausted and elated over our accomplishment, we talked about the day before crawling into our sleeping bags.

Early the next morning, we began the trek down. It was a brutal descent. The weight of the backpack pushed me forward. My shins ached as I tried to steady myself on the downward-sloping trail. In some places, it felt as if one misstep could send you hurling off the trail's edge to the canyon below.

***

An immense wave of satisfaction filled me as we arrived back at Whitney Portal.

We loaded the car and drove to the town of Lone Pine, a few miles away. The one restaurant there, popular with climbers before and after a climb, is where we had our first full meal in three days—giant burgers with large wheat buns, fries, and Cokes. We scarfed it all down before beginning the four-hour drive home.

A few minutes into our ride, I began to get an uneasy feeling—the same kind of uneasy feeling that had landed me in the hospital before. Bill and Dick were in the front seat, engaged in spirited conversation about the climb. I was in the back, suddenly feeling faint and weak. My breathing slowed dramatically, and a flush of heat erupted across my body, now itchy and red. A shiver ran up my spine, and my head dropped. I was out.

They had no idea. Some thirty minutes passed before my eyes eased open. My gut quivered.

Dick turned around. "You're finally awake," he said with a light chuckle. "You were completely out."

"Yeah, I know."

We continued our drive back to LA as I looked at fading red marks on my arms.

FINALLY AN ANSWER

It was the last weekend of July, anniversary time. Pat and I decided to spend it in Palm Springs, California. Heather and Donovan were home for the weekend.

"July in Palm Springs," our friends warned. "You must be crazy. It'll be a hundred and ten degrees."

We brushed their comments aside, insisting the cool hotel pool, balmy nights, and lack of crowds would be a welcome change from the hustle and bustle of LA, with its summer tourists, packed beaches, and strangling traffic. Also, I had just produced another series of videos for a client and looked forward to a short break before starting the next large show.

Because of its charming small-town atmosphere, Palm Springs had always been a favorite getaway spot. It's about a two-and-a-half-hour drive east of LA, in the low desert. Despite the heat, Pat and I felt we could survive for a long weekend. After all, it was our anniversary.

Driving late at night, we sped along I-15, and the farther we went into the desert, LA radio stations began breaking up with static. We searched for others and picked up one of those powerful clear-channel, 50,000-watt stations back east that could reach audiences across the country when local stations signed off. I knew about them from my early days in radio.

The show we picked had an all-night male host, who was taking music requests from listeners. It was like in the movies: *Play Misty for Me* or *Sleepless in Seattle*.

I said to Pat, "You want to have some fun? Try giving him a call."

"You're kidding," she said with slight chuckle in her voice.

"No, really, go ahead. It'd be fun to see if we can get on the air. Tell him where we're calling from and where we're going."

She reached for the phone, called the number, and gave the screener on the other end of the line our names and information.

Pat held the phone for several minutes. She turned to me and rolled her eyes. "See? We won't get on."

Just then a radio voice said, "Welcome back everybody. It's time to take some calls. We have a couple calling in all the way from California."

Pat and I stole a glance at each other. I smiled. Her mouth fell open.

She quickly held out the phone toward me.

"Hello, Ed and Pat," said Ron, the enthusiastic all-night radio host. "You're on the air. Tell us what you're doing in California this late-night hour."

My blood was pumping fast, probably from the sudden shock of talking to a nationwide audience of listeners. I decided to play along. I took the phone.

"We're driving through the desert in Southern California on our way to Palm Springs," I said, "for our anniversary."

Pat stared at me with wide eyes.

"Wow!" he said. "On your way to Palm Springs. It must be pretty warm there. How hot is it?"

I laughed. "Tomorrow it may get up to 110 degrees."

"A hundred and ten degrees? I bet you'll be spending a lot of time lounging in the pool."

"Yes, that'll be on our list of things to do for sure."

I stole a quick glance at Pat, who was nodding and nearly laughing.

"For your anniversary," Ron asked in a slow, soothing, low radio voice. "What special song can I play for you two lovebirds in California?"

We rolled our eyes. I thought, *You've got to be kidding me.*

I said, "How about 'That's All' by Johnny Mathis? That was a favorite when we met in college."

With a fake whisper, he said, "Okay, for Ed and Pat driving through the hot California desert, this is for you."

We heard the beginning of the song, but the radio signal turned static before it ended.

"Want to trying calling him back?" Pat asked with a devilish look.

"No. We wouldn't be able to hear him anyway."

We broke out laughing.

"What special song can I play for you two lovebirds?" Pat said, trying to mimic the low, slow voice of the DJ. She leaned over and gave me a kiss on the cheek.

"Don't make fun of him," I chuckled. "Remember, when we met, I was a young radio guy."

"I *do* remember," she said, leaning back in her seat. "But you were in news, not taking music requests on the air."

That little piece of fun broke up the monotonous drive. Just before midnight, we arrived at our hotel in the center of town. The temperature was in the mid-nineties.

***

The next day, our anniversary, we did linger at poolside much of the day before dinner at an Italian restaurant the hotel recommended. With low romantic lights and soft Italian music playing in the background, the evening began with champagne, followed by a wonderful dinner and excellent Italian wine and deserts. I gave in to my temptations with bread and a plate of pasta.

"Be careful of how much of that you eat," Pat warned.

"I'm fine. It is our anniversary."

After dinner, we were off to a late-night club for dancing. People were lined up in front, waiting anxiously for the doorman, whose arms were the size of my waist, to wave them in. We took our place in line and soon received "the wave" from those arms.

It was loud, crowded, and stiflingly hot inside, even more so than outdoors. We sat at a small table that could handle two people but had four huddled around it. The music blared.

We ordered drinks, looked at each other, nodded, and made our way to the dance floor. It was too noisy to talk, too hot and too jammed to really dance, so hand-waving, eye movement, and some swaying back and forth had to suffice as the DJ cranked up the music volume.

In a few minutes, my shirt soaked with perspiration, I leaned into Pat and screamed in her ear, "Let's sit down."

We made our way back to our table, which somehow had even more people squeezed around it. Everyone appeared to be enjoying the atmosphere. Our drinks waited for us.

I'd been in many studio recording sessions but nothing with this volume and bombast. Feeling uneasy, I shouted to Pat, "I'll be right back. I'm going to the men's room."

Pushing my way through the crowd toward the entrance, no one gave an inch as the floor vibrated and seemed to sway. The noise level was intense. The air was thick and steamy. I needed to cool off with some cooler air—any air. I was not feeling good.

***

My eyes eased open. Bright ceiling lights illuminated the hallway. Confusion filled my mind. I was lying flat on the floor, woozy, my head turned to the side. People were watching. I felt hands on my legs and chest. Fire department paramedics were wrapping my body in some type of a cocoon. It actually felt comforting. They worked quickly.

It was loud when I heard Pat's voice cut through the noise. "Honey, just relax. You're going to be okay." She leaned over me. I saw the concern on her face.

My eyes focused on hers. "What? What happened? What's going on?"

"You collapsed," she said, touching my shoulder. "You didn't return to the table. I went to find you and saw a crowd of people around a man lying on the floor." Her eyes teared up. "I walked over and it was you! Oh my God!"

The paramedics carefully lifted me onto a gurney and wheeled me to a waiting ambulance, which took me to the Eisenhower Medical Center. I later learned the "cocoon" they were wrapping around me was a pressure suit, similar to what jet pilots use during extreme flying maneuvers to stabilize their blood pressure.

The paramedics assured Pat that I was going to be alright. She followed the ambulance in her car to the hospital.

By now, emergency room procedures were familiar to me. I was another late-night patient. The nurse went through the routine of checking my vitals—blood pressure, temperature—and asked pointed questions.

I lay bewildered, asking myself, *Why did this happen again?*

The doctor came in, scanned the paramedics' report, looked at me, asked more questions, listened to my heart, ordered an EKG, and left.

It apparently didn't show much as the doctor returned a while later and approved my discharge. I was eager to get up and leave. Pat stood next to the bed, holding my hand, rubbing it lightly.

The nurse came back with some orange juice and said the same words I'd heard the last time this had happened: "Your blood pressure dropped dangerously low, and you passed out. Juice will help restore some of what you lost. Just lie quietly. You'll be okay to leave in a while."

I recalled what the doctor at the Santa Monica hospital had said: "You should get checked out." I hadn't.

An hour later, I was discharged. Pat carefully drove us back to the hotel, asking several times, "How are you feeling?"

Trying to dispel her concern, I said, "I'm okay," touching her arm. "Don't worry,"

My heart rate picked up as I agonized over possible causes for these episodes.

As I woke the next morning, the sun was bright, and the weather forecast called for another sizzling hot day. I smiled at Pat. "How about going to the pool for a swim?"

She looked at me, shaking her head. "I don't think that's going to happen. We're going home."

Still stunned by the episode the night before, Pat took the wheel for the drive back to LA. Her eyes looked red from lack of sleep.

***

When we arrived home, Pat remained upset. I'd previously ignored the doctor's suggestion to be tested for allergies. Carrying our bags into the house, I reminded her again, as I had several times during our drive, "The doctor didn't say I had allergies. He simply said to think about getting tested."

"So, what do you want?" she said, glaring at me. "Someone to hold your hand and take you to the doctor?"

My body tensed. "No, not at all."

"Then what?"

Growing irritated, I softened. "Look, I realize I need to find out what's going on. . . ."

"Then *do* something, for God's sake. You have a family to think about."

"Of course. I know that."

"Do you really?" Her voice was thick with sarcasm.

"I can't risk passing out in front of clients."

"Who cares about the damn clients?" Her voice choked. "You could die. Do you ever think about that?"

"Don't worry, I'm not going to die." I tried working up a grin. "I just need to find another doctor."

I set her suitcase down on the bed. Before she unzipped it to begin unpacking, she looked at me with pleading eyes. "Why don't you call Dr. Khalsa, who I've been going to? He could help you."

Dr. Khalsa was a holistic Sikh doctor in Beverly Hills. The doctors in his group were MDs who also practiced holistic medicine.

"What do you have to lose?" she said. "He knows what he's doing."

I was skeptical but agreed reluctantly to call him and make an appointment.

The first thing I noticed when I walked into the reception at his office was how quiet it was. Everyone spoke in low voices. When I said, "Good morning," the receptionist's eyes widened.

She sat up with languid movements and, forefinger to her lips, said, "Good morning," almost in a whisper.

"Sorry," I said, lowering my voice.

Maybe she'll start humming, I thought. This was not the typical medical office reception full of commotion.

161

The exam room was more like a warm, comfortable office than the usual cold, sterile four walls. It had two chairs and a small cabinet in the corner. On top of it sat a blood pressure sleeve, a box of rubber gloves, Kleenex, and a flower. There was a live plant sitting in the other corner.

Dr. Khalsa entered wearing doctor whites, but it was his white turban I found unsettling for some reason. I didn't know much about holistic medicine and was suddenly suspicious about this whole environment. Pat had told me the doctors wore turbans, but I was still stunned seeing it. "Be open," I recalled her saying. "I think he's good."

He's a medical doctor, I reminded myself, *not just someone dressed in white about to go into a trance.*

He talked quietly and with confidence, quickly scanning my medical history on the documents I had completed at the front desk.

"You indicated you've had several episodes of passing out," he said. "Tell me about those."

I told him about the latest episode in Palm Springs and what I could recall about the earlier ones. I had brushed those off initially, but the frequency had picked up. He jotted notes before setting the papers aside to put a stethoscope to my heart and check my blood pressure.

Leaning forward, he said, "Let me have your hands." He took hold of them. "It's important for you to slow down and relax so I can read your body."

Read my body? What's he doing?

We sat there for a few minutes as he felt pressure points on my hands, wrists, and arms.

"Breathe slowly," he said quietly, eyes closed. "You're not relaxed. Something's bothering you."

I thought, *I'm not here for a shrink appointment. I just want to find out why I'm passing out.* Doubts rose in my mind. Was this just another wasted doctor visit?

He opened his eyes and let go of my hands. He made a few more notes on his chart, looked at me, and said, "I'll be back in a moment." He stepped out of the room.

A few minutes later, he returned carrying two small brown bottles.

"These are herbs I'd like you to take," he said, handing them to me. "They have plenty of natural ingredients to strengthen your system as we explore why you're having these fainting spells." He sat down. "I'd like you to write down and keep track of everything you eat and when you eat it for the next ten days."

Clearing my throat, I asked, "Do I need to take allergy tests?"

"No," he said. "I don't think that's necessary at this time. Our methods are somewhat different. We want to understand what's going on in the *entire* body before issuing a diagnosis. Also, write down all your physical activities and how you felt during and after doing them." He quickly added, "If you feel any dizziness, stop what you're doing."

No other doctor had told me to log my food intake and activities. I was feeling more confident about his method and followed his instructions, cutting out all wheat-related products and a few other foods in the process. It wasn't easy. The herbs helped cut down my anxiety.

I saw him every other week for six weeks with detailed lists of everything I'd eaten and done. Each time he gave me more foods to eliminate and went through the ritual of listening to various points in my body. My patience began to run thin for an answer, any answer.

At home, Pat was encouraging. "I just know he's going to get to the bottom of this," she said. "Do what he tells you."

Just as I was about ready to give up on him as I had with other doctors, he said, "I've studied everything you've provided these past weeks, including how your body reacted to various food restrictions. There is no doubt in my mind you have a severe wheat allergy."

I was transfixed. My first feeling was one of satisfaction—a definitive statement. No "maybe, possibly, could be."

What did it mean? I sat listening intently as he calmly continued.

"Under severe stressful conditions, with the wheat in your system, it reacts with hives, rashes, and swelling. When you add intense physical activity, exhaustion, and open pores, it's the perfect storm. Your blood pressure drops, and you could collapse."

"That happened to me at least four times," I said anxiously.

"You've been lucky so far," he warned. "But it could turn into anaphylactic shock when your tongue swells and your breathing passages close down."

"No one ever mentioned that to me before," I said, startled.

"You need to eliminate food that contains any trace of wheat," he said, looking at me for a reaction.

There was doubt on my face that he must have picked up because he peered back, and his calm voice took on a harsher tone. "Trust me!"

Whoever heard of not eating wheat—bread, crackers, cakes, pasta, and all those good things? Just how limiting will it be with these allergies?

If saying it was serious wasn't enough, to emphasize the point, he prescribed an EpiPen kit to inject myself if my throat began to close.

I was hopeful leaving his office, but deep inside, a dash of skepticism remained.

Pat was thrilled I'd followed up with Dr. Khalsa and had religiously followed his instructions the past several weeks, leading to a conclusion and a plan in place for the future.

***

Cutting out wheat for a few weeks was relatively easy, but not eating it at all concerned me. I had to wrestle with my diet.

At the time, gluten-free was not something people talked much about. Asking for gluten-free in a restaurant or at the grocery drew blank stares. I had to find alternatives.

The temptation to try food with wheat was ever-present. When I slipped up, sure enough, I had a reaction. It got to a point where if I just looked at a piece of bread, a quiver would go up my spine. "I can imagine my throat closing if I had any of that," I told Pat once.

"Well, you're not going to have any," she'd say firmly, "so get it out of your mind."

The herbs helped slow and balance my system. Even those I worked with noticed a difference. Bob, my writer friend I'd known for years, mentioned it more than once. "Ed, you seem calmer these days." He seemed almost suspicious. "What's going on?"

CITY BOY or FARMER

It was the beginning of the nineties. A ceasefire had been reached in the Persian Gulf War. *Dances with Wolves* and *Silence of the Lambs* lit up movie screens.

My business was moving forward with success. At one time or another, I had done work for at least eight major corporations. Growing with existing clients was more efficient than spending time and money scouting for new ones, so I decided to limit my search efforts. Additional clients might have meant more income, but it also could have meant more stress, time away from family, and less freedom to do things I enjoyed doing.

Dr. Khalsa, who pinpointed my wheat allergy, once told me, "To relieve stress, you'd do well if you lived outside LA in a smaller community."

I dismissed his comments. "That sounds good," I said, "but that's not where my clients and contacts are."

On an occasional weekend, Pat and I did manage to get out of town to Temecula, about ninety miles southeast of LA, where my sister Irene and her husband, Clark, lived and worked as real estate agents. With its agrarian landscapes and vineyards stretching across its eastern side, Temecula had come to be known as wine country. The western side's rolling hills, however, were saturated with avocado groves. It was an area labeled by locals as "up the hill."

Perhaps fittingly, my brother-in-law, Clark, had the gift of gab. He was friendly to everyone and a good salesman. He never lacked for words when giving me a point-by-point rundown about what was selling in real estate, especially avocado groves. Once, he grinned and said, "Ed, you should own an avocado grove."

I laughed. "Sure, all I need is another headache. I have enough of those running my business. Farming is not for me."

Yet every visit, he seemed to persist. "Come on. Let me show you some of the sprawling avocado groves up the hill."

"Clark," Irene said, somewhat annoyed, "they came for a visit, not to drive around looking at trees."

Pat had no problem with it and simply said, "Oh, go ahead."

There's no harm going for a ride, I thought, and we'd be off for the next hour driving by groves with Clark expounding on the advantages of owning one. The passion in his voice was obvious as he played tour director.

Simply out of curiosity rather than any real attraction to owning a grove, I said, "I don't see too many avocados on those trees."

His breathing increased as we stopped in front of a grove. "The fruit is there," he said, eager to elaborate, pointing to the trees. "It's camouflaged by the green canopy of leaves. Look closely."

I studied the branches for a moment, my eyes scanning left and right, looking for any sign of avocados.

"Oh yeah, I see them. But not very many."

He chuckled. "Oh, this grove is loaded with fruit alright. The owner lives nearby and uses a small crew of farmworkers who keep it healthy with the watering, fertilizing, and everything else it needs to be sure it's producing good fruit."

"Sounds like a lot of work to me," I said, staring out the car window at the large, lush trees, some nearly twenty feet high, neatly spaced apart, running up the hills as far as the eye could see.

We drove back to the house, where Irene stood at the door with a wide grin.

"What'd you think?" she asked. "Ready to be a grove owner?"

"No. I'm a city boy, not a farmer," I answered. "But Clark is quite persuasive and seems to know all about groves."

"He should," she said, shaking her head. "He drives around them almost daily with potential clients."

Clark also sold homes, but he was more comfortable talking with grove managers about trees and land than sitting in an open house.

***

Several weeks passed, and Clark's poking and prodding continued. I was becoming a bit annoyed myself. Clark was talking about avocado groves every time we visited them. Then I made a casual remark. "Maybe if the right grove came along, I'd take a look at it. It has to have healthy trees yielding a profit, with little hand-holding needed on my part."

His ears perked up. That was all he needed. Two weeks later he called, sounding excited.

"A friend of mine just put up for sale one of his two avocado groves," Clark said. "It's five acres with over a hundred and fifty healthy trees and plenty of room to add more. I think it'd be a perfect investment."

As he took a breath, I thought, *Owning a grove is not in the front of my mind or a priority. At work, we are deep in producing a series of videos for a client.*

Clark didn't let up. "Maybe we can look at it. When will you be coming out again? I think it may sell fast."

"Right now, it's impossible for me to think about anything but work," I said, reminding myself, *I know nothing about farming.*

"This grove could yield a good return," he insisted. "It's on a paved road, up the hill in an area with multimillion-dollar estates. It's a prime location."

I had to admit, the way he described it did pique my interest.

A week later, on a warm, sunny day, I journeyed out to Temecula, skeptical but willing to look.

"You need to get the feel of the earth," Clark said as we pulled up to the grove.

We got out of the car and walked into the trees. He spoke with confidence, knowing exactly what to point out to move a potential sale along. The deeper we ventured into the grove, the more comfortable I began to feel. A quick shiver went up my spine for a moment as the dark green Hass avocado fruit revealed itself, hanging under the lush fullness of the leaves. A light breeze ruffled the treetops. I weakened a bit, thinking, *Maybe I could handle a grove. He did say it would be a good investment.*

"These trees are mature and healthy," Clark said, brushing branches aside. "They'll produce an abundance of fruit and a good return. Oh, and one other thing: this grove has pad in the center, and has passed the perc test."

"A what?"

"Let me show you."

We walked to an open, flat clearing, where he stood, looking proud. I saw nothing but a large patch of land surrounded by trees.

His face lit up. "Where we're standing is about ten thousand square feet and can be the site of a home one day—if you want to build," he said.

Scanning the area, I asked, "What does 'perc' mean"

"That's when the soil has been tested to determine its absorption rate, which is vital to properly design a septic system, if a building is planned. Some of the hills in the area won't pass the test."

I felt the tug of a grove but also felt the tug of my business and family.

We walked back to the car and pulled out a couple of bottles of water from the trunk. As we stood there enjoying the cool drink, a pickup truck passed by. The driver waved. Clark returned it.

"Someone you know?" I asked.

"No, it's just what people do in these hills. Everyone's friendly and watching out for each other." Clark's attention turned back to the grove. "I know the grove manager who takes care of this grove. He's terrific and keeps it producing."

Another car passed. The driver tooted his horn and waved.

"I live ninety miles away," I said, narrowing my eyes at Clark. "Distance is a major deterrent. I'm a hands-on guy and couldn't be this far from the site."

We talked for a while before wrapping up, and as I drove home, my mind was flooded with thoughts, not the least of which were about the costs of owning a grove and its earning potential.

I had built up a small cash reserve in my business for emergencies and wasn't about to jeopardize it by jumping into a business I knew nothing about. On the other hand, letting cash sit in the bank wasn't a good long-term plan either.

***

Back home, I talked with Pat.

"You don't know anything about farming," she said with a small grin. "Clark often makes things seem rosier than they are." She tilted her head to the side. "Are you sure you would want to work with avocadoes?"

"No, I'm not, but it's intriguing to think about owning an income-producing piece of property. It would be owned by our business."

"If you really want to do it, make a very low offer," she said. "You can always increase it."

Clark called me a few days later. He didn't waste time wanting to write an offer.

"Look," I said cautiously, "if you can get the grove for 15 percent below the asking price, I'll consider it."

There was a pause, and he let out a deep sigh. "That's pretty low. The owner might be insulted."

I thought, *Who are you working for, me or the seller?*

"See what you can do," I responded, slightly irritated.

There was hesitation in his voice, and I felt some tension between us as we hung up.

I told Pat about the offer and Clark's response.

"Be careful," she said. "He tends to hyperbolize, but I think Irene will call him on it if he starts doing that. She's on your side."

Clark wrote up the offer and presented it to the seller. Three days later, he called me. I was at work, thinking about everything other than avocado groves.

"The seller won't accept your offer," he said, "but did counter, saying he'd split the difference. That'd be a good deal."

Not surprised my long-shot offer would not be accepted and still not 100 percent certain I wanted to own a grove, I told him, "Let's not pursue it."

He sounded stunned but tried to maintain a positive tone. "I can talk with him again."

"Do what you think is best, but if he wants to sell it, that's all we can afford."

A couple weeks passed. I hadn't heard anything and was sure it was over when Clark called.

"I saw the owner of that avocado grove yesterday," he said. "He seems anxious to move it. Have you given it any further thought?"

"Not at his price," I said. "Look, I'm busy at work. The thought of owning a grove was nice but not realistic. Let's drop it."

I heard the resignation in his voice when he said, "Okay."

A few days later, the phone rang again.

"Hi, Ed!" Clark. "If you want the grove, he'll agree to your price."

Apparently, he didn't drop it, I thought.

The pressure was back on me. I had decided to move on but blurted out, "Give me a few days to think about it."

"We don't want him to change his mind," he said.

"Well, if he does, he does," I snapped. "I won't be pressured."

"I'm not doing that," Clark insisted, sounding defensive.

***

Pat and I talked. I called Steve, our accountant, and even talked with the grove manager in Temecula who Clark recommended. He gave me his opinion.

Things were moving fast. The next day, I called Clark, my mind racing.

"Okay, let's do it," I said, a light quiver in my stomach. "Make the deal."

Forty-eight hours later, I was the nervous and anxious owner of an avocado grove—or "ranch," as the farmers called them.

It was a major challenge to run two separate businesses, one of which I knew little about. I was an absentee owner, paying a grove manager and his crew to take care of it. This was diametrically opposite to my way of operating, being present and on top of everything.

There was a whole new set of terms and conditions to learn: avocado sizes (24's, 36's, 48's—those sound like measurements for something other than avocados), snail damage, 5-5-5 fertilizer, tree skirting, water meters, weed hacking, fruit pickers, trucking, packinghouses, packing fees, door charges. It was somewhat overwhelming.

What had I gotten myself into? How could I balance this with my usual business?

For the first several months, I eagerly made the drive nearly every weekend to talk with Dick, my grove manager. He'd been caring for groves in the area for over twenty-five years and was very matter-of-fact and unemotional in telling me what needed to be done to keep the grove producing marketable fruit.

There were many things to learn about farming, and I had other challenges demanding my attention.

A TV DOCUMENTARY

In one stretch of about fourteen months, a deluge of work came our way. We wrote and produced some twenty product videos of various lengths for my RV client, plus a large national dealer show. It was a staggering amount of work with sixty-hour work weeks, and it burned me out.

Pat encouraged me to take a break. "Look, you've been working nearly nonstop for months. It's time to do something you'd enjoy without the pressure of a client."

"It isn't easy to pivot on a dime," I said, mildly irritated.

At the time, I was deeply involved with coaching youth ice hockey. Several times I overheard a couple parents talking about the learning difficulties their kids were having in school. One of them said her son was diagnosed with dyslexia.

"Our doctor recommended some special education at a school called Landmark West in L.A.," she said. "Class sizes are small and the faculty has advanced degrees in special education. He started this semester, and I'm excited about the overall progress he's made so far handling the many issues he's dealing with." She took a breath before adding, "Playing sports like hockey is a good outlet for him, they told me."

Intrigued hearing them talk, I wanted to learn more about dyslexia and learning difficulties. Could it could affect young athletes following coaching directions. How?

I contacted Joan, president of the Southern California chapter of the Orton Dyslexia Society, a nationwide organization that provided information and support services.

Joan was friendly and invited me to meet in her Orange County office. I could hear the passion in her voice as she meticulously outlined the challenges young and old go through with learning differences.

"More people should hear about this," I told her during our meeting.

"I agree, but we have limited resources to get the information into the hands of those who need to see it."

Over the next few weeks, the conversation with Joan lingered in my mind. Ideas kept popping up in my head, like ducks in a carnival shooting gallery. I hunted for some way to help spread the word.

One idea kept resurfacing in my mind: a TV documentary. Even before my early days as a journalist, TV documentaries had captivated me.

Mentioning it to Pat, she said, smiling, "It sounds like a great idea, but how are you going to do that?"

"Don't know," I responded. "An idea is one thing, but turning it into reality is another."

I decided to run it past a couple TV distributors in LA whom I'd met in my earlier venture into TV with my travel series. They might be open to some funding.

"It's a PBS-type program," one insisted from the depths of his plush Beverly Hills office as he tilted his head back rather dismissively. "There's not enough interest in the subject for commercial stations to pick it up."

In short: no money to be made.

Another distributor told me point-blank on the phone, "When you have a completed show, I'll look at it. Beyond that, I can't offer any help."

It was discouraging and frustrating.

Determined to find anyone who might offer financial support, I mentioned it to one of my corporate clients.

"It sounds like a wonderful idea," he said, "but not something we can help you with. Good luck!"

***

Without financial help, I was having second thoughts. *Where would the time and money come from to write and produce it myself? Do I dare try?* Business had improved, but this would be much different from the corporate shows and videos I produced.

The avocado grove was turning a small profit, but I still had to keep a watchful eye on it. As long as my grove manager was there, I didn't need to be on site as much.

Joan, for her part, could put me in touch with experts around the country who could speak about the subject, but she couldn't do much else.

"It's not looking good," I told Pat one night while we were out for a walk.

She reached out to take my hand. "You'll figure it out."

"I'm not as confident as you are. It'd be expensive and time-consuming to produce it on my own."

With a warm, knowing smile on her face, she said, "I know," and we continued walking.

My clients had no large-scale productions on the calendar, but if something came up, I couldn't afford to shortchange them and potentially lose them to a competitor while I was doing something else. It was their continued support and steady work that allowed me the freedom to even think about producing a risky independent documentary.

Torn about what to do, weighing the best- and worst-case scenarios, I decided to run the music and tell the story.

***

Unlike many TV programs, where the entire script is written before production begins, this documentary would work off a broad outline and a synopsis I wrote based on research into the stories we aimed to tell. In one sense we were running blind, not sure what we'd hear in various interviews, but this wasn't a make-believe drama. It was real life, and flexibility was key.

We needed parents, teachers, and experts versed in learning differences, along with, of course, young students experiencing these problems themselves.

Doubt clouded my mind. *Did I miscalculate what it's going to take to pull this off?* It would take time to gather data, do research, line up interviews, schedule, negotiate with production crews, and keep in contact with my corporate clients.

Joan mentioned Caitlyn Jenner, Bruce Jenner at time, was dyslexic. My pulse began to race.

"It would be great to have him as part of the show," I said. "He's a face everyone recognizes. Do you know how to contact him?"

She responded casually, as if it were no big deal. "I have a phone number."

Excited, I called the next day and left a voicemail. The following day, we connected and talked about the program. He was happy to tell his story on camera. A week later, we went to his home and set up for the interview.

He was relaxed, casually dressed, and gracious in his Malibu living room that overlooked the ocean. Pat, whom I wanted to host the show, engaged Bruce in conversation for nearly an hour about being dyslexic.

Sitting comfortably opposite her on a white sofa, he said, "My greatest gift in life, looking back, was being dyslexic. It started me off knowing that I wasn't going to get something for nothing. I would not have won a gold medal if I weren't dyslexic. It taught me I'd have to be disciplined and work extra hard to achieve my goal. I turned my learning difference into a positive for me."

His appearance was what we needed to help bring attention to the issue. I was thrilled.

***

Joan mentioned a multimillionaire real estate developer in Orange County who hadn't learned to read or write until he was in his forties.

I called him. At first, he declined to be interviewed on camera about his learning problems. The longer we talked about how helpful it would be to others, he agreed to appear.

John was in his mid-fifties. He and his tutor, who'd taught him to read at age forty-eight, had been to the White House as presidential guests.

He welcomed us into his spacious home with a warm smile and friendly manner. As the cameras rolled, Pat talked with him about his struggles. She has a talent for getting people to relax and open up.

"When I was going through school, teachers weren't reaching me with their standard teaching methods," he said. "They put me in the dumb row in grades three through six." His eyes watered, and he turned away from the camera, trying to control his emotions. "Sorry," he said with a big swallow. "I turned to sports and eventually went to college on a basketball scholarship and graduated. Believe it or not, I taught high school social studies for eighteen years after college."

Pat responded with a look of disbelief on her face. "You went to college, then taught school and couldn't read? How?"

"Tenacity," he said. "I taught to my strengths—debates, discussions, and presentations."

***

Despite the stories we were hearing, it wasn't enough. I wanted to demonstrate to the viewers what it feels like to learn differently, especially as a dyslexic. I brought in a highly skilled learning specialist to set up assignments that students might do in a classroom.

For the demonstration, our students consisted of eight adults, including Pat, most with college degrees. None had any learning problems. To draw attention to the issue, all the words in their assignments were backward!

Our cameras rolled as these adults attempted to complete several lessons in a prescribed amount of time. Frustration grew. One of the "students," Bruce, was having such a difficult time. He got up and threatened to walk out. "This is silly. I can't do this," he said, looking into the camera.

Our instructor made condescending comments young students might hear from teachers in front of the entire classroom: "Have you been doing your homework, Bruce? Who can help Bruce with the first letter? We've studied that word for months now, Bruce. You need to try harder."

He glared at her, red in the face. "I'm trying as hard as I can." He regained his composure and sat down.

The highly charged simulation left others claiming, "I felt stupid and dumb." "It was impossible to follow along." "It took me so long to figure out some words."

The learning specialist said, "Now you can see what some kids in school must feel, those unable to grasp what's placed before them, who are often criticized, humiliated, or called dumb."

***

I was pleased with the simulation and more so when we were allowed to film in real classrooms at Landmark School. My worries whether the children interviewed might freeze up when the camera rolled disappeared when they didn't. And none of the students felt a leaning difference was going to hold them back in life.

"I want to go to Harvard," one eleven-year-old told us.

Another twelve-year-old added, "I want to be a doctor."

Another said confidently, "A lawyer."

Their positive attitude was amazing as we witnessed teachers work their magic.

"These kids are smart, intelligent, and creative, with high potential," the teachers told us. "They often lack self-esteem from being put down in previous learning situations. We work with them to restore it. These kids are courageous and determined."

Our footage and the number of stories were mounting. After each day's taping, I began paper editing late into the evening. Paper editing is spending hours and hours viewing tapes, selecting takes and comments, writing code numbers, and essentially building the show on paper before going into the expensive Hollywood editing bays costing hundreds of dollars an hour.

The documentary began to take shape. Meanwhile, balancing my time was becoming a challenge. I feared being spread too thin, engulfed in three separate businesses. One was taking care of my important corporate clients, another dealing with avocado farming, and the third producing a TV show. Plus, I had a family at home to take care of.

***

Joan encouraged us to talk with a judge in Jefferson Parish, Louisiana, a well-known and respected expert on the subject of learning differences. Cautious about the mounting costs, my camera crew and I boarded a plane to New Orleans.

I told Paul, my cameraman, "Let the camera roll even if the interview seems over. We don't want to miss anything. I'll tell you when to cut."

When we arrived, Juvenile Court Judge Thomas McGee stood behind his large mahogany desk to greet us. Full of law books and framed certificates and degrees, his chambers projected power and authority. Two heavy leather chairs sat before his desk, and a lone family photo sat on the credenza behind it. Across the room stood a small conference table.

Judge McGee looked serious yet approachable. He was middle aged and had thick dark hair with a tinge of gray, high cheekbones, brown eyes, and a friendly smile. He was dressed in a dark suit, white shirt, and tie.

The judge was animated during our conversation. Holding up a pamphlet, he said with a slight southern drawl, "There have been studies that prove the kids we adjudicate as delinquents are twice as rich in LD [learning disabilities] as the normal population of kids." He dropped the pamphlet on the desk and sighed. "Some kids simply can't learn in the traditional ways being taught in school," he continued, "so they fail and are going to be judged a failure, a dummy, or lazy."

He paused, took his eyes off of me, and peered into the camera. "Nobody wants to be a dummy. They'd rather be bad, so they drop out and are on the bricks with all kinds of other people. Shaking his head, he said, "We see kids in a total state of despair because they can't succeed in school. By the time we get a kid thirteen or fourteen years old, the devastation is often done. Their ego has been shattered."

The interview had gone on rapidly for nearly forty-five minutes. He glanced at his watch and shifted in his chair. "Sorry, but it's about time to get to court."

The camera kept rolling and followed him as he stood up and took a few steps toward a clothes rack holding his judge's robe. He removed his suit jacket, hung it up, and reached for the robe.

"Some of these kids have difficulties with authority," he continued, slipping on the robe. "Not because they want to be a smart aleck or want to give the police officer a hard time. Some of these young people have difficulty comprehending verbal language and what's being asked of them. Some have trouble with sequencing."

He finished buttoning his robe, reached for his collar, and straightened his tie.

"When we're in court, watch me try to ascertain if the young person appearing before me might be having some difficulties."

I noticed he didn't use the words "disability" or "dyslexia."

There was a soft knock on the door. His clerk stepped in. "Excuse me. We're ready, Your Honor."

**

In the juvenile courtroom, I stood next to the camera in the back.

The courtroom was small. The American and Louisiana flags stood behind the judge's bench. A court stenographer and clerk were seated on the right side of the bench. In front of it was a small conference table. Sitting on one side was a fifteen-year-old girl, her parents, and her advocate attorney. On the other side sat two people from juvenile hall.

The proceedings felt very personal.

When the judge asked the girl to raise her right hand, she raised her left. "Your other right hand," he said. She paused and raised her left again, then her right. When asked for her name, age, and address, she appeared to stumble, answering in reverse order.

The judge darted a glance at me as if to say, *See what I mean? I told you.*

While in New Orleans, we interviewed a suburban school superintendent and parents who'd experienced the challenges of coping with their child's learning differences. The parents' perspectives added another dimension to our story, although the superintendent's comments struck me as more political than really answering the question about what schools can do to help students with learning differences.

***

Returning home, following two days of interviews, I felt confident we gained new insight to tell our story. I wrote the final show and worked out lower rates with the video editing facility in Hollywood. This helped with the budget, but a conflict raged within me when it came to the critical decision of who would be the second on-camera host. Could I afford a celebrity? In my gut, I knew it needed an identifiable name on the screen.

A few years prior, actor Edward James Olmos received an Oscar nomination for his role as the mathematics teacher Jaime Escalante in the movie *Stand and Deliver*. This was a powerful story about an LA math teacher who inspired his students to overcome challenges, persevere, learn calculus, and pass the AP exam. Olmos's name and face recognition had appeal. He would be a perfect fit. But would he do it, and for how much?

My pulse raced as I called his manager (bypassing his agent), whose name I received from the actors' union. He agreed to meet.

On a hot, muggy, smoggy day, with the temperature hovering around one hundred degrees, I drove to Universal Studios in Burbank. The hum of the air conditioner was a welcome sound as I walked into the small two-room bungalow on the lot to meet him. He had an easygoing manner and carried a slight New York accent.

185

"Tell me more about your show. When are you shooting? Are you producing it? What would you want Edward to do?"

I spent the next thirty minutes filling in the details and answering his questions.

Sitting behind his small desk, his shoulders back, he said, "It sounds interesting. I'll pass it on to him. What will you be paying?"

He didn't sound optimistic when I told him five thousand dollars. "He'll only be working one day," I quickly added.

"He usually gets a great deal more."

"It's a documentary," I said, "about kids and others struggling every day."

"I understand," he said, sounding impatient. "It sounds like a wonderful show. I'll make sure he has all the information."

We shook hands, and I walked back into the searing heat.

Two days later, he called me. "Edward agreed to host but would need more money to do it."

My heart sank. My mind raced. *What do I do? Be careful! Watch your costs. Don't let emotions enter into it. You knew he might ask for more.* I took a deep breath.

"He won't be asking for any special accommodations on location, will he?" I asked.

"No. He'll bring his own assistant to handle anything he needs and will show up ready to work for as long as you want him that day."

We went back and forth until I said nervously, "Okay, let's do it." The minute I said that, my second-guessing began: *Am I paying too much?*

"It's still below what he normally receives," the manager went on, "but since it has to do with children, he agreed to take less."

We were taken by surprise when, at one point during his on-camera segment, Olmos revealed that he too was dyslexic, adding even more authenticity to the program.

The passion he and Pat brought to the program was unmistakable. One was dyslexic, the other a parent of a dyslexic child. They knew what they were talking about.

***

The compelling hour-long documentary, titled *Kids, Dreams, and Courage*, aired on PBS stations across the US—often repeated—and on selected broadcast stations. NHK, the giant Japanese television network, purchased it for broadcast on their vast system, and it reached audiences as far away as Guam. We received scores of calls, faxes, and letters requesting a copy.

I felt a swell of satisfaction and warmth spreading through my body knowing we'd touched people lives. We'd helped them gain a better understanding of the personal and silent difficulties many live with every day.

In the midst of completing this documentary, the question of whether I could mount this project while keeping my corporate clients happy and my farming business successful was answered.

GIVING BACK

I was standing in the ice rink watching young players come out of the locker room and head for the ice to warm up for their forthcoming game when Joan rushed up to me, a little out of breath. She ran the youth hockey program at the rink. Like a den mother to the kids, she had an easy smile and a caring attitude towards them. She knew I played the game and that Donovan played on the team taking the ice.

"Hi, Ed," she said, looking stressed and talking fast. "I've got a problem and wondered if you could help me out."

"Sure," I answered. "What's up?"

"The coach for tonight's game just called and can't make it. We can't start without someone behind the bench. Would you be able to take his place?"

"No problem. Happy to do it," I said.

Her shoulders dropped, and a smile spread over her face. "Great. Thank you."

I walked to the bench and briefly talked with the players, and the game began. It was easy, and I enjoyed it.

***

A few months later when we were registering Donovan for the next season, Joan hinted about the shortage of coaches and floated a question my way: "How would you feel about being a regular volunteer coach for one of our teams?"

With at least one practice and one game a week, how would I balance it with my business pressures? I was out in Temecula checking on my grove at least once a week. I was busy working on the TV documentary and at the same time planning another corporate show for a client.

Concerned about the time it would take, I told her I'd think about it. A few days later, I agreed under one condition—I could coach Donovan's team. I was taking him to the rink anyway. She agreed.

Joan didn't initially mention that volunteer coaches had to be certified by USA Hockey and attend a day-long certification seminar. The seminar laid out what was expected from a coach: training young players, planning and running practices, handling games, and the latest rules. Each coach received his associate certificate upon completion, meaning we could coach USA Hockey–sanctioned teams.

Being a volunteer coach carried responsibilities beyond standing behind the bench during a game. At 6:30 a.m. Saturday morning practices, a dozen or so young players stood waiting for my instructions that would, hopefully, ideally turn them into a winning hockey machine. Well . . . maybe not a machine but at least a team. Parents sat in the cold rink, bundled up as if they were in a refrigerator. They watched intently, hoping their son would stand out and I wasn't playing favorites.

***

In games with players below the age of twelve, bodychecking was not allowed, although players did get "accidently" knocked down. Games were played in running time, meaning the clock didn't stop for face-offs and penalties unless a player was hurt.

My team at the time was made up of nine- and ten-year-olds. We had one player, Tommy, who, while not the best player, was determined and ready to do anything asked. He wore very thick round glasses behind his face mask and smiled a lot.

One Saturday morning, we were playing a game against a team across town and leading by a single goal in the final period. We hoped the clock would run out and we'd win the game. I told the players, "Take your time coming off the ice and, if knocked down, get up slowly."

Late in the game, Tommy was knocked flat onto the ice. Parents in the stands gasped when he didn't move. The referee gave me the signal to go on the ice and check him. He was sprawled on his stomach.

I got down on my knees. Placing my hand softly on his back, I asked, "Tommy, are you okay? Are you hurt?"

Without moving the rest of his body, he turned his head toward me. His thick glasses magnified his blue eyes, and he whispered, "Am I taking enough time? Should I stay down?"

The referee, standing there, asked, "How's he doing?"

"He's alright," I said.

I turned back to Tommy. "It's okay. You did just fine."

He slowly got up and skated over to the bench as the parents in the stands applauded.

We eventually won the game. During my postgame talk in the locker room, the players sat there, helmets off, faces glowing with perspiration running down their foreheads, their eyes wide as saucers, all looking excited and healthy, awaiting my approval.

"We played very well today," I told them. "Every player gave it his best."

My eyes caught Tommy's as a shy smile lit up his freckled face.

***

I enjoyed coaching, especially upper-level double A and triple A teams. They required intermediate- or advanced-level coaching certification, awarded at a two-day seminar.

At higher levels, players and parents demanded more—more practices, more games—and for me a thicker skin. It wasn't unusual to be cussed out or threatened by parents for not playing their child enough or for playing a kid they thought wasn't very good.

"We lost the game because you played our backup goalie!" a father screamed as the team walked to the locker room. His son looked embarrassed. Pointing his finger at me, the father added, "You're a son of a bitch and don't know how to coach. I'll see you outside in the parking lot."

After the players dressed and left the rink, I wondered if the upset father would be in the parking lot. Somewhat apprehensive, I went out, but he had gone. His son probably didn't want another embarrassing outburst.

Getting screamed at seemed part of the job being behind the bench.

***

Coaching hockey, playing myself in an adult hockey league, and keeping my businesses moving was a balancing act. It didn't leave much time for anything else, but that didn't stop the club from asking me to be their representative at the monthly league meetings in Southern California. Although hesitant, I agreed.

Over the next couple of years, this led to being elected to the league board and then to the state board of directors, the governing body for amateur hockey, as well as sitting on the executive committee as first vice president, handling disputes from across California. Any serious violation of rules would land in my lap. The amount of work increased dramatically. I thought about stepping down.

Being a volunteer was gobbling up my time. Arriving at my office on Monday mornings, I'd be greeted with emails, faxes, and phone calls about incidents in games over the weekend, everyone demanding some action or a formal hearing. My secretary, Flossie, who had been working with me for nearly ten years, often ribbed me as I sat running my hands through my hair, trying to sort out a hockey dispute.

She'd smile. "You're just a volunteer, right?"

"Yeah," I'd say, often frustrated.

***

Donovan had one more year to play before aging out of youth hockey. He was invited to join a Midget AAA team in Madison, Wisconsin. The team played in one of the elite leagues in the Midwest. It was coached by former Olympian Bobby Sutter.

It was his senior year in high school. Pat and I agreed to have him attend school in Madison and billet with a local family. The hockey was good, but we could have done better with the billet. Both of the adults worked, and neither were home at the end of the school day.

Once we became aware of his situation, we insisted on moving him to a different billet. With the help of the coach, we did, and it was a perfect family setup in a home with four kids and parents at home. His grades and hockey improved.

He returned to LA at the end of the season and graduated from high school here.

After a year in junior college, Donovan transferred to San Jose State University, where he played on its hockey team for three years, being named captain the last year.

After graduating, he worked for me on a couple live corporate shows, but his heart was into sports, and he was hired as a staff sports producer at the NBC TV station in LA. From there he landed a job at Fox Sports producing live TV sports.

Heather in the meantime was working at Universal Studios, where she met her future husband. Heather dated several guys, and the closest we got to meeting any of them was a wave from their car when they came to pick her up or drop her off at home.

Then she met T Paul, and things changed.

"Wait until you meet him," she said with excitement in her voice. "We're going out Saturday. Will you be here?"

Pat said, "Sure. We're looking forward to meeting him."

That evening at eight, the doorbell rang. I answered it.

A good-looking man stood there, smiling. "Hello, I'm T Paul."

"Nice to meet you," I responded. "I'm Heather's dad." We shook hands. "Please come in."

Pat came into the living room, and he introduced himself to her.

T Paul was amiable, good looking, and a gentleman.

We chatted for a few minutes before Heather came into the living room, glowing. She was talking fast, I suspect hoping that our meeting him for the first time would work out. It did.

A short while later, they were on their way out. "Have a nice evening," we said.

I turned to Pat after they'd gone. "He's nice. It's good to see a guy come to the door for a change."

"Yes, I know," Pat remarked, shrugging. "Maybe Heather just wasn't serious enough about any of those other guys for us to formally meet them."

"Could be," I said.

MEETING THE CHALLENGES

After years as an independent producer hoping for steady clients, I now had plenty of work to keep me busy. My confidence rose with the smooth flow of business, and I was determined to keep expenses low with a lean staff and quality service at the highest level.

Always a keen eye on sales opportunities, my Realtor brother-in-law, Clark, let me know the avocado grove next to mine was now for sale and had "about four hundred producing trees," and "it's turning a profit for its current owner," he crowed.

Cautious about another outlay of money, I repeated what I'd told him before buying the first grove. "I'm not sure. The grove we already own is taking more time than I imagined trying to keep it profitable. I'll talk to Steve, my accountant, and run it by Pat to see what they think."

Steve was his usual conservative self, telling me to move slowly, but he didn't say not to do it. Pat was supportive, knowing we were making a small profit with the grove we had.

Feeling anxious but excited about the prospect of owning two groves, I called Clark. We went back and forth with offers until we came to an agreement with the seller, and we now owned another grove, hoping Clark was right about its profitability.

Meantime, my largest client at the time was still a leader in the RV and manufactured housing industries. Over several years, I had built up a strong working relationship with Earl, the vice president of its RV group, and others in the company. They didn't accept every idea presented but relied on my judgment more often than not regarding their meetings, shows, and product videos. I made it a point to try to be in their offices at least two times a week. Being visible, reliable, and steady was important.

Changes were in the works, however, which increased my anxiety.

Larry, the RV director of marketing, whom I'd also worked closely with, was leaving to join a competitor company in Indiana. He was replaced with Bill, someone internally whom I knew but had not worked directly with before. He came out of their sales department and had a friendly demeanor, and I got along well with him. The transition was smoother than if they'd brought in someone from the outside. His style was to make quick decisions, delegate, and not interfere much once the work had begun. I produced their next product launch show in Las Vegas and the following year, one in San Antonio. We worked well together. It was at the latter meeting that Earl announced his retirement. This was a major change, and a shiver went up my spine. Who'd be replacing him? I was extremely disappointed and worried about what his leaving would mean. A month later, they announced the general manager from one of their manufacturing facilities, whom I'd never met and had no connection with, would be taking his place.

Uncertainty filled my mind. I wasn't sure how it would affect my business, but the new VP appeared set on bringing in his own team, as corporate executives often do. He wanted to transfer Bill to a new position. Instead, Bill decided to leave. They hired a new marketing director with no experience in the industry. He was a young gun, so to speak. My gut told me more changes were in the works.

Time was short before their next product show and launch. I'd already presented a proposal before he had been hired and followed through producing the show in Washington, DC.

Arriving for his first major address to dealers, the new guy proved to be as lightweight as I'd suspected, barely finishing his script before his moment onstage. To salvage his presentation, my on-site crew worked well into the early morning hours the day before the opening. Despite the last-minute commotion, the two-day event came off well thanks to my experienced show team.

A few months later, my silent fears turned into reality. I was completing a series of videos for them when they told me they were going to "go a different direction" on the next product launch—as in they were going to use a different company.

I felt an urgent need for some internal support and asked the vice president of product design, whom I had known for years, to put in a good word for me. To my dismay, his response was noncommittal. He'd always been supportive before, but now, when I needed it the most, he shriveled up. I suspect because the company was changing, he had his own turf to worry about. I was shaken to the core losing what for nearly twenty years had been my largest and most consistent client.

Who would replace them? The smaller clients I was working with didn't generate enough income to fill the void.

I had learned long ago to conserve and not overspend when times are good because one day things may turn the other way. They did. At home, we had a small cash reserve to help carry us through for a short time if needed without having to make drastic changes to our lifestyle. At work, I pulled the belt tighter.

You bet on yourself and triumphed over adversity before, I reminded myself. *Well, here you go again.*

I got busy making calls to other potential clients.

***

Meantime, Dick, my avocado grove manager, mentioned a new term I'd never heard before: "root rot," an agricultural disease that attacks avocado trees and ultimately kills them. There's no set pattern either. It'll attack one grove and miss entirely the next one over.

"What about our groves?" I asked Dick as we stood in the groves assessing the situation. I was wary his answer might not be a good one.

He assured me he was on top of it. "I'm keeping my eye on them and see no sign of it."

I was relieved but not entirely satisfied.

The two avocado groves were marginally profitable, but the small profit wasn't nearly enough to replace my largest client.

At home, tension grew between Pat and me. "You're very irritable," Pat said more than once as we cut out travel and trips of any kind, pulled back on eating out at restaurants, canceled the twice-a-month gardener, put off replacing my old car that had 140 thousand miles on it, and basically spent more time looking for ways to save.

It didn't cost anything to go to art openings, and we enjoyed going together. It was important for her to stay in touch with what was going on in the art world and build important contacts to further her painting career. I fully supported her.

Kiddingly I said, "You'd better start selling more paintings." As an accomplished painter, she spent every available moment working on a new canvas. As her acting career slowed, her art career gained recognition. She exhibited in galleries and museums throughout Southern California.

"Museums don't sell paintings; they just exhibit," she reminded me with a smile.

***

Root rot continued to rampage through many avocado groves in the Temecula area and eventually didn't spare ours. The disease is in the soil and difficult to detect at first. It moves silently, killing trees slowly, and can be carried from grove to grove by coyotes or other animals running through them and also be on grove workers' shoes.

Dick spotted it in our groves when the leaves began shrinking and falling, leaving sparse, small, and unmarketable fruit.

I had to spend more time at the groves working with Dick to develop a strategy to save the trees. We tried everything, including injecting them directly with special fertilizing formulas recommended by nurseries. We increased watering, trying to "wash" the soil, hoping it would heal itself. Then we heard the soil needed to be dry, and we reduced watering.

Nothing worked.

Gradually, over a season, all that remained on one grove was nearly four hundred bare, dying trees. Few survived, only to die the next season. My other grove lost 60 percent of the trees, and those surviving barley produced enough fruit to pay the expenses. It was heart-wrenching to see.

Clark had sold me the groves several years earlier when there was no sign of the disease. I held no ill feelings toward him, but now we were talking about possibly selling them.

"With the root rot and dying trees, you probably won't receive anything near what you paid for them," he warned. Grove owners in the area were turning off the water and letting their remaining trees die rather than trying to keep them growing. Some growers were selling.

After months of calls and letters to the county regarding property taxes, I achieved a small victory. They agreed to lower the property taxes slightly, noting the value of the groves had shrunk without the marketable fruit on them.

I made the difficult decision to remove the dead trees and replant. No one could guarantee the soil was clear of root rot if we replanted avocados. We switched to grapefruit, which is not susceptible to root rot. The cost of removing a tree, buying another, and planting could have amounted to between fifty and sixty dollars each.

Constant worry filled my mind. "Organic fruit would return more money," Dick said confidently as we walked together through the groves, inspecting the trees.

It takes three years to be certified organic, requiring costly organic fertilizers, organic farming methods, and carefully kept logs of everything we were doing in the groves. I also had to pay for annual organic inspections by licensed certifiers. It still baffles me sometimes why we replanted rather than simply taking the loss and selling.

Though going organic did increase my income, it wasn't enough to cover the expenses. There was a great deal of cash going out and very little coming in. It was a delicate balancing act. The question that occupied my mind was *Why did I ever get into owning groves?*

I was in a deep money pit.

***

My corporate business shrunk to nearly nothing, and I was down to one full-time employee, Flossie, my dependable assistant and office manager. She was the first voice anyone heard when they called and provided a sense of continuity. Clients got to know her as much as anyone who'd worked for me.

Our long list of freelancers we'd used were still available with a phone call.

Sitting alone in my office, I stared out the window and spoke to the glass about looking for a staff position at another media company. It would be a crushing personal defeat, going backward.

Just as everything looked bleakest, I received a phone call from Larry, the former marketing director, who a couple years earlier had left my then-largest client. He was now the division president of a large publicly traded RV company.

Grateful and surprised, I listened as he extended a lifeline, asking if I would be interested in coming to

Wakarusa, Indiana, a place I'd never heard of, to discuss the first-ever national dealer show they were planning. With a surge of hope, I immediately answered "Sure," booked a flight, and was off to Wakarusa a few days later.

He didn't offer a guarantee of any work or if they'd pay my expenses for the trip, but I had no choice. I had to go. Unless I could secure some work from them or other clients, my days as an independent producer would be numbered.

The one successful formula for my dealing with a client had always been visiting them three or four times a month, more if they were local. I wanted to demonstrate to them they were important to me even when not producing a current video or show.

However, this potential new opportunity in Indiana was a couple thousand miles away. How much hand-holding could one muster from that far away? I decided to make the effort.

Following lengthy conversations with Larry in his Indiana office, I returned to LA, wrote a creative proposal, and flew back to Indiana to present it in person to him and his executive team. They liked what they heard and asked me to produce the show. Even though to start, their business would amount to less than half of what I had lost, there was an opportunity to grow. I was excited and desperately needed the work.

Dealing with a client across the country would be a new adventure. They had high expectations, and thankfully they were satisfied we met them. The show was a success. No one cared if I had a large staff. That was a signal I didn't miss. They only wanted assurance the job would be done well. This changed my thinking.

Some corporate clients I had worked with questioned how service could be kept high with only a small staff. "It's not the number of people but the quality of the people you have that make the difference," I'd answer and follow with a question: "The DMV has many people in their offices. How'd you like *their* service when you go in?"

Walking through my offices, I decided there would no longer be a costly large full-time staff. When needed, I would call any one of the many excellent and dedicated subcontractors whom I'd worked with for years.

This is getting back to the basics of keeping overhead low while keeping quality and service high, I told myself. *It got me to where I am and will continue to do so in the future.*

***

The previous two years had been the most challenging and nerve-racking since setting out on my journey. Slowly emerging from uncertainty, my new client looked positive for the long term. Meanwhile, the grapefruit were not affected by any lingering root rot in the soil, and organic farming of the fruit was yielding slightly more returns.

I had renewed energy. The key to surviving for me had always been to stay balanced, focused, and financially conservative. There are always going to be good times and bad; be prepared for both. Toughing it out was the right decision.

26.2 STAY HEALTHY

The travel and time demands required to develop and hold on to my new client three quarters of the way across the country were new to me. I was used to seeing clients frequently and couldn't in this situation. My worrying and tension increased, wondering if this new client would last with my not being in front of them often enough.

Is there any truth in being "out of sight, out of mind"? Time would tell.

Being goal-oriented had always been a key to success for me. If I had a target to aim at, my mind didn't dwell on other problems. Never one to sit idle, I often turned to physical activities to relieve stress.

An article in the newspaper caught my eye. The LA Road Runners, a running group, was beginning to train for the LA Marathon, nearly six months away. Much as my mind wondered about possibly rock climbing again, I couldn't escape the thought, *What would it be like to run a marathon?* Saturday morning training sessions "open to anyone," the article said, were held at a school four blocks from my office in Venice. Curiosity got the best of me. I had to check it out.

There were at least 150 people, everyone from teenagers to seniors, registering at the several tables set up in the school courtyard. Some looked like experienced runners: lean, matching running shorts, tops with logos of some race they'd been in, good-looking running shoes, running watches, water belts, headbands, and self-assured attitudes.

No one pushed for a commitment to sign up, and that suited me.

Inside, the school gym had a small stage at one end. Amid the Bengay-scented air of excitement, runners maneuvered for a position to hear the orientation talk by the coach on this first day of training. Some sat on the floor near the front and others in folding chairs. I stood in the back. Conversation echoed throughout.

"Quite a crowd," I remarked casually to the young guy standing next to me.

He nodded. "Seems like running a marathon is very popular."

"Have you run one?"

"No." He gestured to his lean friend nearby, wearing a Road Runners shirt. "My buddy Jay has, though."

"Looks like you've done this before," I said to Jay.

"Yes I have. It's my third year. How about you?"

"I'm not much of a runner," I answered haltingly. "Just curious."

At that moment, a cheer went up as the coach entered the room with a bright smile, waving.

He stood about five feet ten inches tall, was lean with salt-and-pepper hair, and was dressed in running shorts, a Road Runner T-shirt, and white tennis shoes. He was a former high school running coach and competitive runner who'd competed in the Olympic trials once. He bounded onto the stage with high energy.

"Over the next twenty-six weeks of training," he said bright-eyed, gesturing to the Road Runners logo behind him, "the LA Road Runners program will make sure you're ready to compete when the gun goes off in downtown Los Angeles."

The room erupted in cheers, smiles, and high fives all around. Confidently walking back and forth on the stage, the coach continued, "If you follow the training program, I guarantee you'll finish the race." Another cheer went up. He reminded me of a motivational speaker I'd use in a corporate show.

Could I finish a marathon? The coach believed anyone could. At least anyone there. And I must say, his enthusiasm, and the crowd's, began to reach me as he spoke for nearly half an hour.

"We'll meet Saturday mornings," he said, "and our training run will increase each week by a mile until we reach twenty-two miles."

What am I doing here? I can't run twenty-two miles, or even two.

"In addition," he continued, pacing back and forth, "you'll be running Monday through Thursday on your own with a schedule we'll provide."

The crowded gym hung on his every word. "We have a cadre of experts to talk to us about the health and physical aspects of training, including hydration and diet."

Some heads turned when he mentioned diet.

"Yes, diet. You'll be burning a tremendous number of calories every week, and your body will be stressed, especially as the miles increase."

Running five days a week? This isn't for me. Work alone keeps me busy nearly sixty hours a week.

"Let's get to our first morning run," he said with vigor and excitement in his voice. "We'll walk to the Venice Beach Boardwalk, our starting point."

I turned to Jay. "Good luck."

"Aren't you coming?"

"No. I haven't signed up and don't think I can run a marathon. And these old tennis shoes aren't running shoes."

"Oh, come on. It's only a short run this morning."

"I've got to get back to work. Have a good run."

As the crowd of runners shuffled past, I stood watching when a voice in my head took over: *You came here to see what's going on. Give it a try. You don't have to run. Just walk!*

Taking in a deep breath, I turned to join the runners.

***

The weather was in the sixties, perfect for a morning run along the beach. As I stood among the excited runners, my nervousness began to turn into competitiveness. I told myself, *If everyone else can do this, maybe you can too.*

Apprehensive, I stood near the back of the large pack. My adrenaline was flowing.

"Well, here we go," I said nervously to the runner next to me, bending side to side.

"Yep" was his only response.

Raising his voice, the coach reminded everyone, "Run at your own pace. Pacing is what will get you to the finish line, not trying to outrun the person next to you or sprinting out to fast."

It crossed my mind how similar this was to running a business. It demanded the same disciplines: pacing, determination, dedication, perseverance, and the will to achieve your goal. A well-balanced goal suited me.

Dragging myself to finish that first morning, even though it was only a mile, was tiring, but I felt satisfied.

***

We were supposed to run Monday through Thursday, starting with a mile each day. Not sure I'd return the following week, I ran a short distance just in case.

The next Saturday, the crowd hadn't thinned out. The registration tables were busy. I saw Jay, the more experienced runner, but didn't see his friend.

"Where's your friend?" I asked.

"He decided to skip today," Jay said.

"But it's only the second week. . . ."

"I know." He shook his head. "You can't run a marathon without putting in the work, including every Saturday. Oh well."

To me it was like working for yourself. You need to be consistent, and show up every day.

The coach took his spot onstage to "fire us up." Invigorated, he announced, "Two miles today."

My stomach turned. *Two miles?*

Somehow I did it, actually walking most of the second mile. We returned to the gym for the lecture about running shoes and taking care of your feet.

By the third week, I'd made up my mind and paid the training fee, which included the entry to the marathon. After that morning run, I went home and told Pat about my plans.

"You're what? . . . Marathon?" A look of total surprise washed over her face as she stood there looking at me in disbelief. "Why?"

"That's what I've been asking myself," I said with a slight grin. "It's something, relatively speaking, few people have attempted. I've been training with the LA Road Runners Saturday mornings for the last three weeks."

"Oh?" There was a rise in her voice. "So that's why you've been going out for a 'short' run every night?"

"Right. Sorry I didn't tell you sooner, but I wanted to be sure rather than just talking about it."

I told her about the program but couldn't yet imagine the enormous amount of time training would take.

"Be careful," she said with a slight shake of her head. "Running on hard payment will take a toll on your entire body, not only your legs."

That week, I bought new shoes and running shorts and was starting to feel like a real runner.

***

The training was grueling. The distance increased each Saturday, heading toward the goal of twenty-two miles before tapering three weeks before the marathon. My body urged me to get more sleep, eat less junk food, and pay close attention to pain. Experienced runners had a light, easy running gait. Mine was more of a heavy jog.

Balancing and scheduling my time with practice runs was a constant challenge. There were days I was racked with guilt, running after work rather than being home with Pat. More than once during those runs, I entertained the idea of quitting. This was taking a great deal of time and energy.

It soon became apparent that it's not possible to finesse your way to completing a marathon; it takes work. Even when traveling out of town to see my clients, I'd put on the running shoes at the end of the day and run. I felt like Forrest Gump.

As part of the training regimen, we ran in 5K, 10K, and 30K races.

"Running these races," the coach said, "is where you'll learn what it feels like to stand shoulder to shoulder with hundreds of runners waiting for the race to begin. You'll be anxious, your heart will be pumping fast, and you'll have the urge to sprint off the starting line once the horn goes off. *Don't!*"

***

The night before the marathon, I stayed at the hotel the Road Runners had reserved four blocks from the starting line as I didn't want to face morning traffic on race day. Excited, I laid out my running gear on the bed: shorts, socks, T- shirt, energy bars, running belt, hat, sunglasses, running bib with number, and pins, plus a change of clothes for the end of the race.

I didn't see my running shoes. A shiver went up my spine. Where were they? Panicked, I quickly searched every corner of the room and went back to my car to look for them.

I'd left them at home!

The coach constantly reminded us to make a list of everything we'd need for a race and to be sure to check it. It'd take me nearly two hours to get home and back. I needed to rest and frantically called Pat.

"What?" she blurted out, almost with a chuckle. "You forgot your shoes? Didn't you make a list of what to take?"

Annoyed and impatient, I said, "Yes I did."

"Did you read it?" There was a touch of sarcasm in her voice. "You need to be more careful."

I'd said that to her in the past, so she took a gleeful moment to rub it in. I was relieved when she agreed to bring my shoes to the hotel.

***

Sleep was fleeting that night, and at 5:30 a.m. the alarm went off. I had prearranged room service for a bowl of oatmeal and orange juice. Wheat allergies prevented me from bread or rolls, which would have helped fill the emptiness in my stomach.

The forecast called for possible rain. I left the hotel in a cold drizzle and nervously walked to the starting corral, where thousands of runners stretched for blocks. It was 6:45 a.m.

There was an air of anxious energy around me as I slid into the huge crowd of excited runners. It was surreal. My heart was pounding. I closed my eyes, trying to relax. That didn't work. Questions filled my mind: *Am I ready? Can I do this? These runners look better than me. Should I move back?*

Excitement filled the air as the start time approached. It seemed the huge crowd of some twenty-five thousand runners had tightened up, with some runners moving forward as if a couple of feet would make a difference in their time.

I was too far back to see the platform at the starting line where race officials, including the mayor, made a few welcoming remarks. Then, just as I'd done so often in my corporate shows, they ran the music, signaling the race was about to begin. Randy Newman's "I Love LA" blared over the loudspeakers.

A roar erupted.

The horn went off—the race was on.

The massive throng inched forward. My 26.2-mile journey began with a goal of just finishing.

After the first couple miles, the crowd of runners spread out, each running at their own pace.

The coach had told us to stay hydrated with the water stations flanking the street at every mile marker. Twenty to thirty volunteers in yellow jerseys stood at the stations, their arms extending paper cups of water. I grabbed one, drank it, tossed the cup, kept running, and reached for another.

This isn't too bad, I said to myself at the nine-mile mark, taking it all in as thousands of spectators lined the course, shouting encouragement.

At twelve miles, our coach stood in the middle of the street. He raised his fist for a high five. "Keep going, Road Runner!" he screamed. His words gave me a lift.

The heavy clouds opened while I was running along Hollywood Boulevard in Hollywood at about sixteen miles. The rain began. Exhausted, with heavy legs and aching feet, I threw my head back, thrust my arms into the air, and took in the raindrops. The quick downpour was refreshing. It ended in ten minutes as the sun emerged and the temperature rose.

At eighteen miles, questions returned: *Why did I think I could do this?*

Eight miles to go.

Water lost its taste. The Gatorade I carried on my runner's belt was too sweet. My stomach was upset, and I was depleted. My slow stride turned into a battle to keep putting one sore foot in front of the other. Feeling miserable, I ached to sit down and fought the urge to give up.

***

Turning the corner at mile twenty-one, the course flattened out a bit. The hazy LA skyline could be seen far off in the distance. My spirits shot up. There were thousands of us still on the course. The elite runners and veteran marathoners had already finished and were probably enjoying their postrace rituals. Spectators thinned out except near a water station or in front of one of the small strip malls that dotted the course.

To keep motivated, I engaged in my own separate race, targeting a runner ahead of me, telling myself to pass them. Once that was accomplished, I picked another to pass. The twenty-two-mile marker across the road was in sight, along with a water station.

"Keep going!" cried the volunteer water workers. "You're almost there!"

I grabbed a cup, took a small swallow, grabbed two more and poured them on my head. The cool water running down my face and neck was invigorating for a few seconds.

As I strained my eyes for the next mile marker, my mind was foggy. *Where is it? Maybe there isn't any marker for mile twenty-three, or they're putting them only at every other mile now. It sure feels like we've run another mile.*

In reality, we'd just gone a short distance from the last marker, twenty-two.

The sun peeked through threatening rain clouds and warmed my back. My shirt hung dry on my shoulders. I'd stopped sweating miles ago. My hands and ankles were swollen.

I saw a marker. *That must be mile marker twenty-four.* A moment later came disappointment as mile twenty-three came into focus. I skipped the water station and kept going. My legs were simply moving logs. Three miles to go!

Mile twenty-four brought a gradual downhill slope. *Thank goodness.* I heard nothing, smelled nothing, tasted nothing, and could see only the towering skyline growing closer.

Running through downtown LA's canyon of high-rises, making the final turn toward the finish line less than a half mile ahead, I was jolted awake when the PA announcer proclaimed, "And now, turning the corner is number 17142, Ed Tar!"

The size of the crowds increased again, as did the cheering. I swung my arms a little higher, trying to pick up my pace. Dehydrated, hungry, entranced, and concentrating only on finishing, my heart burst with surprise and excitement when I saw Pat standing on the curb, screaming and waving. She hadn't said she'd be at the race. How'd she know when I'd be rounding that corner? She broke through the crowd and came onto the course, running a few strides with me. "You look great!" she called. "Keep going! I love you! See you at home!" With a smile, she returned to the sidewalk.

The finish loomed just two hundred yards ahead. Above the finish line, stretching across the road, was a bridge full of dozens of photographers snapping photos as runners crossed below. A large digital timer hung below it. Shaking, feeling proud, tired, and emotional, I focused on the timer the last hundred yards. With my arms high in the air, I threw my head back and let out a roar as I crossed the finish line. A photo captured the moment.

My body, heavy with the weight of what I'd just done, stopped moving as an excited volunteer placed a medal around my neck.

"Congratulations!" she said. "Are you okay?"

Wobbling, I managed a slight smile. "Yes." They handed me a tin foil blanket for protection from the wind and drizzle.

Shivering in the cool weather, with dead legs, I dragged myself the four blocks back to the hotel ballroom that was reserved for Road Runners to change clothes after the race. I crashed onto the ballroom floor and lay there for a half hour before struggling to change. My feet had swollen within my shoes. In nothing but stockings, I slowly made my way to the elevator and down to the parking garage, unsure exactly where I'd parked.

**

A few months later, when it was time to begin thinking of starting to train for the next marathon, Pat surprised me by saying she wanted to run a marathon. She had always been physically active either at the gym or with yoga, swimming, or anything to keep her body moving.

She joined the Road Runners program, and we both completed the training for the next race. Other than the Saturday morning class and runs, we didn't train together during the week. I usually ran at night after work, and she ran earlier in the day.

We stood together at the starting line. She was nervous and apprehensive. I knew the feeling running it the first time. She did extremely well in her first marathon and decided to run the next one with the Road Runners. She did better and beat me to the finish line. After the second race, her knees ached, and she vowed never to run another marathon.

**

I went on to train further with the Road Runners and run a total of ten LA marathons plus scores of 5K, 10K, and half marathons, logging a conservative estimate of about six thousand miles, the equivalent of running to New York and back. But the emotions of the first marathon would never be duplicated.

Acclaimed author Joyce Carol Oates, who taught one of my college English lit classes at the University of Detroit, once said about running, "If there is any activity happier, more exhilarating, more nourishing to the imagination, I can't think of what it might be."

I ran ten marathons and it solidified something I'd always believed: nothing is impossible with hard work and discipline.

Following the last marathon, determined to keep my health and maintain physical fitness, Gold's, an iconic gym in Venice less than ten minutes from my office, became my go-to place every morning six times a week before work. Founded in 1965, its walls are filled with photos of swole weight lifting and bodybuilding champions, including one of its earliest and most famous members, Arnold Schwarzenegger. Arnold, often there pumping iron keeping in shape, is serious about his health. Seeing him work out and occasionally alternating on the same machine gave me a close-up opportunity to pick up a few tips. Always friendly and easy to talk with, he's an inspiration. The gym courts many Hollywood celebrities, sometimes difficult to recognize in their gym clothes, without makeup.

ART ADVENTURES

Confident the worst was in the rearview mirror with my media business and groves, I turned to Pat while at dinner one evening.

"Honey, we need a break," I said. "We haven't been on a vacation alone in nearly ten years."

She nodded. "That's true."

"Let's get away."

"Okay, I'm for that. What'd you have in mind?"

"How about Italy?"

Her head jerked back a bit and her eyebrows raised. "Italy!" Her eyes widened. "Are you kidding? What about your job?"

Filled with a feeling of confidence about it, I said, "Flossie can handle things at the office. She knows everything and can easily reach me if needed." She had been my right arm for years.

Being in business for myself had always made it a challenge to get away for any length of time. Three weeks was the maximum I felt comfortable being out of my office, and I always made it a point to let my clients know I'd be gone. If they had some project coming up or we were in production, there was no way I'd leave.

Pat broke into a wide smile. "I love Italy. It'd be a lot of fun," she said, her eyes sparkling with excitement. She reached over to wrap her hand around mine. "There are so many places to see. We've never been to Florence," she said, quickly asking, "When would we go?"

"Let me double-check what's coming up at work," I said, returning the smile. "Maybe late summer or early September after the tourist season. What do you think?"

"As long as we go before it turns cold."

Portofino, Italy, a small resort town favored by international jet-setters, had to be on our "must see" list, friends told us. We didn't run in the jet-setter crowd, of course, but couldn't resist, just once, seeing what all the excitement was about.

Portofino sits below the high cliffs of the spectacular northern Italian coastline. It has a small harbor for the yachts of the rich and famous; a few cafés, art studios, and galleries; plus the privacy demanded by its famous guests and international moguls.

Five kilometers from Portofino sits Santa Margherita, a sleepy fishing village with a half-dozen hotels, shops, and restaurants, and a beautiful view of the Mediterranean. Facing the small harbor, one could smell the sea and watch the local fishermen bring in their daily catch. A fifteen-minute walk through town, up past the small train station, stood the beautiful Hotel Continental, overlooking Santa Margherita and the bay below. This was where we stayed.

One morning after breakfast, Pat said, "Let's walk down to town and check out some of the local shops."

"I think I'd rather stay here for now," I said, not wanting to get near any shopping, "and relax at the pool."

Somewhat disappointed, she frowned and said "Okay, I'm going to go for a while." She smiled and left on her own.

During her venture, she stopped at a café for coffee and struck up a conversation with a local, who turned out to be an Italian painter/sculptor. Apparently, he didn't speak much English, nor did Pat speak much Italian, but that didn't seem to matter. They spoke the language of art. She learned he was very well-known in Italy and throughout Europe. His name was Lorenzo Cascio.

Later that morning, she returned to the hotel, bubbling over with enthusiasm.

"Guess what?" she said, her eyes sparkling and words tumbling out. "I met an artist and sculptor at the café in Santa Margherita. He wants to do a sculpture of me."

Eyebrows raised, I looked at her. "You met an Italian sculptor, and just like that, after only meeting a few minutes earlier, he wants to do a sculpture of you? What's the catch? What kind of sculpture?" I cocked my head. "Nude?"

"Of course not," Pat said, looking startled. "I wouldn't do that."

"What, then?"

"It's only from the neck up, like a headshot."

"What'd you tell him?"

She paused and then answered quietly, "Yes."

"You said yes?" My voice rose in disbelief. "Why? What's he going to charge?"

"He didn't say he was charging anything." She took a few steps toward the window and gazed at the town below. "He's going to come by the hotel tomorrow morning, and we're going to his studio in Santa Margherita." She waited for my reaction.

I stammered. "He's . . . what? Coming here?"

Pat turned around. With a warm smile, she reached out for my hand. "Stop worrying. He's fine, and everything's going to be okay." She gave me a hug and soft kiss. "Don't worry."

***

At nine the next morning, the phone rang. Lorenzo was in the lobby. Eager to meet him, I went downstairs with Pat.

Lorenzo was in his late fifties, somewhat bald, with graying hair on the sides and a round face, and a bit overweight. He was about five feet seven inches tall, wore glasses, had a nice smile, and was very polite. He wasn't anything like I thought he would be. In fact, he reminded me of my Italian brother-in-law, John, in Detroit. We exchanged pleasantries.

Her face glowing, Pat climbed into his tiny red convertible and waved as they sped off. It was like a scene out of the Audrey Hepburn movie *Roman Holiday*, but this wasn't Rome.

I spent the day at the hotel worrying. I went for a swim, had lunch, constantly checked my watch, and walked to the front of the hotel several times, looking for a small convertible to come up the hill. Around 6 p.m., it did, and Pat was back.

Entering our room, she was overflowing with enthusiasm and began talking as fast as a jackrabbit.

"It was great," she said, removing her headscarf and shaking out her hair. "You need to see his large studio. It's very impressive. He has sculptures and art all over the place. He wants us to come by tomorrow so you can see the sculpture he did."

Trying to get a word in, I said, "Slow down. He's done?'

"Oh, he just did it in clay," she answered with a wide grin. "If we want, we can have it bronzed."

My eyes widened. "Bronzed?" I blurted out.

She walked to the window. "Isn't this a fantastic view?"

"Did I hear you right?" I chuckled, trying to clarify. "He wants to bronze it?"

Her eyes sparkled with excitement. "Do you know he did a sculpture of Pope John that is in the Vatican? He also did a large piece for his hometown in Sicily that sits in the town square."

Her exuberance was contagious. I found myself curious to check out Lorenzo's studio and the sculpture.

The following day, we made the short trek to his studio in Santa Margherita. Just as she said, it was impressive— fifteen-foot ceilings, large enough to hold many sculptures and paintings. One sculpture he was working on was nearly twelve feet high. Smaller pieces were lined up along one wall.

He walked us over to the piece he'd done of Pat, which was covered with a light cloth. He gestured for us to come around to the front and, with dramatic flair, removed the cloth to reveal the sculpture.

"Wow," I said. "*Molto bene.* It's beautiful."

Lorenzo grinned wide as we admired it from all angles. He insisted on buying us a gelato at the café next door so he could tell us about his gallery in Portofino, where he displayed his very expensive paintings.

The next morning, Pat and I took the local bus to Portofino, about three miles from Santa Margherita. His gallery was equally impressive as his studio. Picking her way through many paintings and sculptures, she came across a small bronzed sculpture of two naked lovers embracing. She negotiated a good price with Lorenzo and bought it.

He mentioned her clay sculpture again, offering to have it bronzed and shipped to LA. I suspected bronzing it, plus export and import duties, would be very expensive. We declined. Frankly, neither of us felt comfortable with a bronzed sculpture of her in our living room. Lorenzo managed a bitter smile before saying, "I understand and will keep it until the next time you come."

***

Several months after returning home, Pat received an email from a gallery inviting her to submit paintings for possible inclusion in a group exhibition . . . in London. I'm not sure how they came up with her name. The exhibition was only three months away.

 Pat was happy about the invite but had doubts. She had received things like this before, and they never panned out. A few days later, realizing there was nothing to lose by responding, she carefully selected a half-dozen paintings, completed her artist's statement, and emailed them. Two weeks later, she received a positive acknowledgement accepting her paintings in the show. She was pleased but still had reservations whether to do it.

"I don't know," she said, studying the acceptance letter. "I'm responsible for getting the paintings there and back."

"We'll find out what it would cost," I told her. "That's easy. Would *you* want to go to London?"

"Ideally, I'd like to send the paintings and also go," she answered with a broad smile. "Maybe we can go together."

"It'd be fun, but I can't travel with the work I have coming up."

She was intrigued and a bit fearful going alone. After thinking it through for a few days, she sent them a thank-you and made the decision to go. We sent the paintings separately.

As luck would have it, our neighbor, a longtime American Airlines flight attendant, was working the flight to London. When she heard Pat was going to be on it, she pulled some strings and quietly upgraded her seat on the way there.

Pat stayed in London for the show. Returning home, she was excited to tell me all about it.

"I loved it there, and being alone wasn't an issue," she said. "I felt like I did when modeling in New York . . . walking or taking the subway everywhere and meeting new people every day."

Her paintings were supposed to come back a month later, but the shipping company made a mistake and sent her paintings to China. She received a crate holding someone else's paintings. It took six weeks of hassling with the LA shipping company before they straightened it out, and she received her paintings.

***

A year later, Pat and I returned to Italy and discovered what would become our favorite place on the Amalfi Coast: Positano, just south of Naples. With its steep rolling hills, small-town atmosphere, and dramatic vistas looking across the Mediterranean, it was the perfect spot to relax or easily adventure to other interesting spots along the coast.

Strolling away from the town center one day, walking up the hilly main road, we discovered a wonderful family-owned restaurant/art gallery, the Mediterraneo. With its walls lined with beautiful original paintings and its food delicious, we couldn't have found a more ideal place, especially for Pat and her love of art.

We stopped there for lunch and soon struck up a conversation with a gentleman at the next table. His name was Peter, a well-known New York artist who happened to be exhibiting his paintings in the gallery. He had been going to Positano for over twenty years and was close friends with Enzo, the gallery's owner/curator. Pat was eager to meet Enzo, and Peter happily introduced us to him.

Enzo, in his fifties, had salt-and-pepper hair, a thin close beard, friendly eyes, and a broad smile. He was an avid art lover. Dressed in a casual open-collar, off-white linen shirt, light tan pants, and canvas loafers, he had a relaxed manner that fit with the setting of the blue Mediterranean in the background.

Pat, ever the loquacious one, soon joined Peter and Enzo to enjoy a prosecco and discuss art. I sat with them, listening for a while, but soon excused myself and decided to continue my walk up the hill.

Enzo and Pat immediately hit it off. "He doesn't speak much English," she told me later, "but that didn't matter. When I showed him photos of some of my paintings, I think he liked them."

We stayed in Positano a few more days and went to the restaurant for dinner each night. The conversation about art continued.

Returning home after our trip, Pat remained in contact with Enzo at his request, emailing additional photos of paintings she was working on.

When we returned to Positano the following year, she brought along a small abstract painting to give him. "It's a different view of the sea," she said, excited. "It may look good in your gallery or in your hotel." Enzo also owned the boutique hotel, managed by his daughter, two doors from the gallery. Pat wanted the painting to be a reminder of her and a gesture of friendship.

Obviously touched and impressed by her artistic talent and dedication, Enzo responded, "I'd like to see more paintings of your American impression of Positano."

Surprised, she responded enthusiastically, "Okay, but I only work in abstract."

"I understand," said Enzo and nodded his approval. "I would like to see how you envision it."

"As soon as we're home, I'll get started on something and email it to you."

With no guarantees, she hoped this might be a first step toward exhibiting in his gallery.

While supporting her, I cautioned she might be wasting her time.

A few weeks later, her first painting, a bright-colored acrylic and oil abstract of the cliffs above Positano, was complete. She sent it. He responded, liking it. He asked if she had anything else to see. For the next two months, she forwarded additional new paintings of her Positano impressions. He always replied positively.

She was growing concerned and was ready to give up, fearing he might be stringing her along. Then one day, I heard a loud scream come from her studio. "Yes! Yes!" Startled, I rushed in and saw her huddled over her computer. "Enzo wants me to create a full solo show at the gallery," she said, her eyes tearing up. Taking a breath, she slumped back in her chair. The tears began rolling down her cheeks.

"When?" I asked.

"Next summer."

She was overwhelmed with joy. I was too, for her.

Over the next year of painting, she completed twenty-four new abstract canvases of her Positano impressions, everything from a romantic, sparkling, moonlit sea to a blazing sun washing the colorful town built into hills, and another of the cliffs over Positano seen from a thousand feet in the air, plus a pair of lovers, hands reaching out for each other as their naked bodies separated, floating over the water.

I cringed at the thought of crating and shipping the paintings round trip. It would cost thousands of dollars. We decided, rather than shipping them, to remove the canvases from the frames, roll them together in what looked like two yoga bags, and carry the bags on board the plane with us. The paintings' stretcher bars were packed in two separate boxes and checked as excess baggage.

It took me an entire day to carefully unmount and pack the paintings. In Positano, they gave me a large empty basement room at the hotel with no air conditioning to remount them. As each painting was mounted, a worker from the hotel took it to the gallery. The process was repeated when the show ended. I vowed never to do it again.

The show's opening was kinetic: fast paced with local media and a large crowd in attendance. We were nervous. Pat was very apprehensive about what the reception for her art would be. Her bright, abstract paintings were in contrast to the realistic, subtle paintings that usually hung in the gallery. Her concern soon turned to smiles as she worked the crowd of guests, engaging them in conversation, talking with the media, and doing what she does best, meeting and enjoying the people. She was in her element.

Italians like Italian art, and a few didn't think anyone's art could measure up to their own, but some were intrigued with an American artist's work.

During the thirty days we stayed in Positano, she sold several paintings. we couldn't have been happier. Included was the painting of the two lovers. It was sold to a young female attorney from Sicily who had escaped to Positano to heal her grief after breaking off with her fiancé.

Although Pat's work had been in international group shows in Basel, Paris, Venice, London, and Tokyo, this was her first international solo show and a high point up to then.

***

During our many trips to Italy, we found traveling *in* Italy never dull.

One time, on a train from Florence to Milan, Pat and I settled into our seats as the train began to move. We looked forward to the relaxing two-hour ride ahead. A few minutes passed when the train conductor, looking stern, came down the aisle with his ticket calculator checking everyone's tickets. We showed him our Euro passes. He looked at them and quickly told us in halting English they weren't valid because we had failed to enter the travel date on them at the ticket window in Florence.

"You must pay a supplement," he said. The "supplement" was twenty-five euros for each ticket, about fifty American dollars total.

Surprised, I objected. "Why didn't the person at the ticket window tell us they needed to be dated before we boarded?"

He didn't speak much English or just didn't care to answer. He shrugged and remained silent.

"I can put the date on it right now," I said, trying to sound polite, "but we shouldn't be charged a supplement."

His voice rose, stammering, "It must be dated before boarding. Not now." He was getting upset.

I told him again the supplement was unfair, adding, "I'm not going to pay it."

Apparently, he felt his authority was being challenged as he blurted out, "If no pay, I will call *polizia*."

He can't call the police on a train, I told myself. His threat raised my blood pressure, and without thinking, I responded stubbornly, "Go ahead, but we're not paying a supplement."

Pat darted a glance at me and, with a slight nudge, quietly urged, "We don't want to get in trouble. Just pay him. Fifty euros isn't very much."

The conductor stood there peering at us, waiting, his chest out, holding his ticket calculator in one hand. A small bead of perspiration formed on his forehead. Nearby passengers took notice of our exchange.

"No. It's unfair," I said again. "We weren't told about dating the passes before boarding."

The conductor abruptly turned and stormed away, very agitated. The train continued on. Thinking the episode was finished, we sat back for the ride to Milan. My stomach was unsettled, though, and my mind raced. *What happens if he* does *notify the police?*

Standing near the door at the end of the car we were in, the conductor watched us as the train arrived at the Milano Centrale train station. The minute it stopped, he rushed off. We reached for our carry-on bags in the overhead rack. Through the window, I caught a glimpse of him talking with two Italian policemen, gesturing to the train and pointing to the ticket calculator he was holding. Pat didn't notice, and I didn't say anything as we shuffled toward the exit with the other passengers. Nervously, I grabbed our suitcases stacked near the door.

Stepping off the train, we took a few steps when one of the bulky Italian police officers approached us. He held up his hand, blocking our path. "Halt," he said with an authoritarian tone. Pat and I stopped. The conductor was pointing to us and talking fast. He must have called ahead, and the police were waiting.

Oh shit, I thought, *we're in trouble.*

"*Buongiorno*," the officer said, somewhat friendly. "The conductor told us you didn't pay the supplement required for tickets not dated."

"The person at the train station in Florence never told us to date them," I pleaded.

With passersby watching, we stood there feeling like criminals being interrogated. Were we going to be arrested for something so minor?

"I offered to put a date on the tickets while on the train," I said, "but the conductor refused to allow it without paying first."

The police officer didn't respond. Realizing we could be in trouble, I reached for my credit card, offering it to him for the supplement.

"We can't accept payment," he said. "It has to be with the rail company."

The conductor stood there wide-eyed as the police explained to him in Italian what I was saying. Their extended back-and-forth exchange was animated and noisy with the conductor interrupting, talking rapidly with sweeping arms, pointing to his watch and the train. The police called his attention to the credit card I was holding. In frustration, shouting something in Italian, the conductor threw up his hands, stole another quick look at the train behind him, and with flaring nostrils and fire in his eyes took a final gaze at Pat and me. He rushed to the train and got on. In a moment, the doors closed as it was about to depart.

Still nervous and startled about the scene we'd just been part of, we stood there, unsure of what would happen next.

"There is nothing we can do," the police officer said calmy. "You offered to pay just now, and the conductor left."

I sensed the two Italian officers were just as happy as we were he had gone. They smiled, said, "*Arrivederci; ciao*," and resumed their slow walk on the platform, watching the thousands of arriving and departing passengers.

Pat and I looked at each other, still a little shaken. We reached for our luggage. "Let's get out of here," I said. The next stop was the airport and our flight home.

ONLY HAPPENED ONCE

As an independent producer, I prided myself on working with solid, often publicly traded large companies with a track record of paying their bills.

The client in Indiana eventually grew into being my largest and remained so for nearly ten years. They were almost like family. I was lucky to have them as a reliable client, and they paid invoices within thirty days with no hassle.

We produced many shows for them, including one in Las Vegas attended by several hundred dealers. It had all the trimmings of a unique corporate event: a large main stage, Vegas performers, live music, sparkling special effects, exciting visuals, videos, executive presentations, and awards. We also produced events in six separate breakout rooms complete with videos, graphics, staging, and effects at the same time.

During the several months working on this show, I had over forty dedicated people engaged in one part of it or another. It was the largest event we'd ever produced for them, and I was very happy with how it turned out, as were they.

Two weeks later, I sent my third and final invoice to them.

Two months passed since the show and still no payment. Maybe it was just needless worry that filled my mind, but for the very first time I could remember, they had failed to pay our invoice by the due date. Adding to my concern was the fact I had already paid all the people who worked on the show, including the Vegas entertainers plus a truckload of equipment we'd rented in Las Vegas.

I called Yvonne, who was responsible for seeing that the invoice was moving through the system for payment.

"I passed it on for payment," she said. "I have no idea what's holding it up. You can call accounting yourself if you like."

That was strange, and I did call accounting but received no satisfying answer from them either. My concern continued. *This is just an anomaly*, I told myself.

The final invoice was nearly three months overdue when I ran into their head of marketing at an industry-wide event. I mentioned the slow payment and my concern. "Do you know what's holding up the payment?" I asked him.

He pulled me aside out of earshot of anyone and quietly said, "Something's going on in the company. I can't tell you what, but stay on accounting about being paid."

This hardly made me feel better.

Returning to my office two days later, I called Mike, the vice president of national sales. He told me the same thing I'd heard before. "I signed off on the invoice several weeks ago."

"Why the delay, then?' I asked, my mind racing and my gut feeling unsettled. "Is something wrong?"

"I'll check on it and get back to you."

He never called back. I tried calling him, but he was always "out of the office."

Larry, my very first contact with the company, formerly head of one of their divisions, was now the special assistant to the chairman. If anyone could dig up answers, he could. He had an amiable disposition, was politically astute and respected, and carried a large amount of influence within the organization. I considered him a friend, having worked with him for over twenty years at two different companies.

I called him.

"Larry, is there any way you could help me out and make a call to find out what's holding up my last payment on the dealer show?"

There was what felt like a minute-long pause before he broke the stillness with an evasive tone, one I'd heard before when he wasn't being fully candid. "I've been out of the loop and don't know anything about it," he said. "Sorry, but I can't be any help with this. Maybe you should try Harold." That raised my concern even more. Harold was the company president, and I've never had to approach any company president about an unpaid invoice.

Stunned at Larry's response, my ribs grew tighter. I thought, *After all we've been through together and what I've done for you over the years, you won't even make an internal inquiry for me?* I sat there silent in disbelief. I'd never experienced this before. His lack of offering any help was a gut punch and added to my skepticism about so-called "friends" in business.

Two days later, nervously pacing my office, I called the company president, who took my call. I quickly explained the situation.

"How much do we owe you?" he asked, sounding morose.

"$265,000," I answered, thinking that would get his attention.

A cold silence emanated from the phone before he responded perfunctorily, "Well, you're not the only one wanting to be paid. There are others, you know!"

What do I say to that? Almost speechless, taking in a deep breath, I said, "Of course, but the show was nearly five months ago."

"I'll look into it," he said and ended the call.

A week later, not hearing back, I placed two more calls to him. No answer.

It crossed my mind, *Is he being dilatory, putting me off?*

A few days later, another call. He answered but was noncommittal. Almost pleading, I said, "I've paid everyone who worked on the show. Could we work out a partial payment?" As a last resort, I added, "How about possibly taking a new motor home in exchange for what is owed me?"

He simply said, "We can't do that."

I was becoming desperate. My stomach quivered. My hand clutched the phone. I paused. I tried to sound as humble as possible. My voice cracked, "I don't . . . I really don't want to get into anything legal about this, but I need to be paid."

My heart was pounding against my chest.

"Well, you have to do what you have to do," he said coldly.

A shiver went up my spine. Sitting alone in my office, my lips began to quiver. I couldn't expel a breath to say, "Thank you."

I dropped my head, muttered "Goodbye," and hung up. My shoulders tightened with his incredulous response. Anger welled up within me as I realized there was a good chance I might not be paid. It felt like a fishhook hanging on my cheek. Was this really happening? I'd never experienced this before.

Warren Buffett once said, "When the tide goes out, you discover who's been swimming naked." Maybe they had been.

***

As tightness filled my chest, I agonized over what to do next. Realizing there was little choice, I picked up the phone to call Todd, my attorney. He'd been a friend for a long time and had handled a couple smaller issues in the past when he ran his own small law firm. But now he was with a large firm in downtown LA, and his fees had skyrocketed. I'd tried to stay clear of calling him and only did as a last resort. This was one of those. We set a meeting to discuss my dilemma.

Walking into the lobby of the large law firm in downtown LA, I began to understand why attorneys charge so much. The lobby looked expensive, and the furniture was leather. The conference room where we met was no different with a long conference table, padded chairs, and crystal ashtrays and crystal water pitcher. It unnerved me a bit as I knew someone had to pay for all of this, and it wasn't the attorneys there.

To add to the uneasy feeling, Todd came in with a young attorney. "This is my associate, Eric," Todd said, introducing me. "If I'm not here, he can answer any questions for you."

All of a sudden, the feeling of friendship with Todd disappeared. I was just another client, nothing more, nothing less. And Eric was another cost to be charged. If we came to an agreement, they'd represent me.

I laid out the contract and what we had successfully produced for the client. Todd took a few minutes to study it as Eric looked on. Todd set it down, removed his glasses, held them between his thumb and forefinger, and leaned back in his chair, his chest out.

"You've obviously done what you said you would for them," he said, "and this looks fine, but . . ." His tone changed. "Before we go on, I need to tell you the standard rate, should you want to use our firm, is one third of the settlement, which is close to ninety thousand dollars, plus expenses."

He must have seen the look of shock in my face when I replied, "Todd, I've done all the work, and attorneys are going to get a third of it for simply filing paperwork."

"We don't know what their response will be, and this could drag on," he said, quickly adding, "I don't suspect it will."

We talked further, and feeling confident it would be settled quickly, he offered a flat rate deal, a fraction of the ninety thousand dollars. Knowing and trusting him, I accepted his proposal.

"It shouldn't take long for you to get paid," he said, glancing over at Eric. "They're a billion-dollar public company, and you obviously fulfilled your obligation as promised." Seeing the concern on my face, he tried to reassure me about the expenses. "We'll be asking for them to pay attorney fees as well," Todd said. I offered a small grin, happy this might be resolved soon and I'd be paid. Eric said nothing during the meeting.

We filed suit in Los Angeles two weeks later. Doing so probably meant goodbye to my client. Even if they paid me, I wasn't sure I wanted to work with them again, and they would probably feel the same way about me.

Weeks had passed when Todd called. The court had set a formal hearing date. My spirits soared.

Just days before the hearing, he called me again with news that felt like a knife to my heart.

"Ed, we just received word the company filed Chapter 7," he said, "meaning they'll liquidate assets to pay off creditors."

"Now what?" I asked, anxiously attempting to glean more information and calm my fears of how it'd affect me.

"If you're going to be paid, you'll need to get in line," he replied with a sigh. "Secured creditors are paid first. If there's any money left after they're paid, usually unsecured creditors are paid. You're unsecured."

A chill went through my body. I swallowed deeply, feeling weakness in my legs. "Those bastards!" I shouted.

"Sorry, but there's nothing we can do," he said.

Trying to remain calm, my hand gripping the phone tightly, I asked, "How long will it take to be paid?"

"It could take years," he answered. "Then it might be only pennies on the dollar. It's up to the bankruptcy court to sort it out."

Idiot, I thought to myself. *How could I have allowed this to happen?*

Word was that the company's banks had apparently cut off their line of credit months earlier, about the time my invoice was received. It would have been only a matter of time before they couldn't pay all their bills.

It was devastating and knocked me off balance. It shook my confidence. My largest client had collapsed and failed to fully pay me.

Sitting in my office struggling for answers, I thought, *What do I do now? Is it time to throw in the towel and do something else?* My mind was filled with many questions and few answers other than quitting, which was not in my DNA.

Determined to not allow this to distract me from my goals, I began placing calls to old contacts. Months passed, with some people telling me the same thing I'd heard years earlier when launching my business: "Stay in touch."

Then, using my farming and grower experience as an entry, I called one of the largest citrus co-ops in the country, based in Southern California. They held a large show with hundreds of growers in attendance every two years. One was coming up. My timing was right. I pitched them, emphasizing my knowledge of the market and their audience. It worked, and they selected me to produce the show. It wasn't as large as I had hoped, but it helped fill the vacuum in my business.

Soon after, I made contact with someone I'd worked with years earlier. He was now CEO of a company developing the first-ever electric motor home. We met in his office several times as he excitedly showed me the concept they were pursuing and how he'd like to produce a film about it and their company.

"This is highly confidential," he said. "Our Chinese backers are a bit paranoid about letting out too much information."

"We've known each other for a long time," I replied, sitting across from him in his office. "There'll be no information coming from me about it."

That seemed to relax him. I presented a proposal to write and produce a video about the company and was awarded the contract to do it.

The Chinese backers came in to screen the final edited video and tour the facility. Tagging along with the tour, I was fascinated when the talk turned to something other than the video or the RV plant we were walking through. I picked up through the interpreter who was with us that they were discussing building an entire new city of the future in China. *Now, that's big thinking*, I said to myself.

***

I was continuing to contact past contacts when my phone rang.

Someone I'd worked with over ten years earlier but hadn't talked with since was now the chairman of a large corporation. He wanted to talk to me about a large product launch and dealer show they were planning. This show would certainly alleviate some of the financial pressure I was under. An overwhelming feeling of gratitude filled my body as we sat down in his office for the first of several meetings with him and his staff. Being a privately held company, they had never done anything the size and scope of what I would propose. They liked the concept and awarded me the contract to produce the event.

Pat and I breathed a sigh of relief. Together, we'd been through several scares and belt-tightening's over the years, and this one was no different.

Energized, Pat wanted to hold a private showing at home to display and sell some of her latest paintings. It grew quickly as we invited friends, gallery owners, and curators. They filled the house and the gallery we set up out back to view her paintings and listen to her happily talk about them.

It was a success. She sold several pieces and was thrilled.

I had to chuckle to myself, thinking, *This "private showing" was almost like producing a small corporate product reveal show.*

Meanwhile, my new client remained steady. I happily continued to write and produce their annual national meetings and shows.

A few years later, I received a letter saying the court was about to dole out what remained of the funds when my client had declared Chapter 7 bankruptcy. I received ten cents on the dollar. Better than nothing but a vivid reminder of how some incompetent corporate executives were lacking the vision and skill to manage their companies successfully

RUN THE MUSIC

Forty years ago, when I started on this path of self-employment, the biggest question that filled my mind was: *Do I have what it takes to succeed?*

I knew I was undertaking an odyssey, one not for the faint of heart, which would require years, if not decades, of determination. There were times I was practically choking on doubt and had to spit it all out—or enough, anyway—in order to succeed, to crawl my way back into the fight.

With some regrets and many successes, I learned a thing or two along the way.

Being successful isn't a solitary journey. Pat and I were a partnership, supporting each other in every step of the way. She was by far my biggest cheerleader. Without her unbroken love and devotion, nothing would have been possible.

Even when her acting career kept her busy, she never wavered in the face of her own challenges to find time to be at my side whenever I needed.

With her second career, painting, on the rise, our time together became even more valuable. Exhibiting her paintings both in the US and internationally, seeing her incremental success in such a tough business, brought both of us joy. She also had my total support in the invisible private moments when she questioned her career, and also in the public moments when her work was on exhibit for everyone to see.

Meanwhile at home, we were often pleasantly surprised when seeing a rerun of some TV show in which she once appeared. Those brought back memories of a period in our lives filled with activity—more auditions for her, --new client shows for me, and the challenges two young kids provided.

***

My personal quest provided the creative freedom and independence I'd always sought. There's no match for the high that comes with completing a successful show or delivering a series of important videos to a client and watching their faces light up with satisfaction and gratitude. I enjoyed the steady hand and focus large, successful corporations provided me, and I resisted the temptation to be sidetracked by the proximity and hoopla of Hollywood.

With the help of a powerful creative team, I was able to produce a body of work, including seventy corporate shows and nearly three hundred videos and films, plus write and produce an award-winning TV series and a TV documentary.

It was exhilarating and rewarding to have the opportunity to work with some of the smartest, most talented and creative people possible. Their skills and dedication made my journey less complicated.

Success can be traced to many things, and relationships played a major role in my ability to carry on every time my demise seemed just around the corner. The people I worked with every day and my clients, even former ones, gave me the hope and the necessary support to fight through to the other side of what at times appeared to be impossible odds. Time and time again, those relationships bailed me out when it seemed my goal—my very dreams—were in jeopardy.

Pick yourself up, dust yourself off, and start all over again were more than just lyrics from the Jerome Kern song "Pick Yourself Up." For me, they were words of encouragement ringing in my ears whenever things got tough and the future looked bleak.

Fear of failing or letting someone down and all the attendant consequences kept me on my toes. As I sat alone in my office, there were times when I wondered just what I was doing. But the thought of quitting and being someone's employee again was not a serious option, although there would be less risk working for someone else. They would have the awesome responsibility of finding and selling a client on an idea rather than I. My role would be what amounts to a staff coordinator.

I'd been there, and it's much easier working in one of those staff positions than accepting the giant risks involved working for yourself.

Reflecting, there was no place I would have rather been than where I was, working independently. *You wanted it; you got it*, I told myself. *Keep moving forward.*

As an entrepreneur, I had the duty and obligation to listen to my clients. I worked twelve hours a day, and it was not unusual to work a sixth day or sometimes a seventh during the week.

Despite all this, there were but only a few regrets. Not thinking bigger, being too cautious, and not taking enough risks stand out as things for which I'd l like a "do-over."

***

I've had the privilege of working with scores of top corporate executives and witnessing what made many of them real leaders, how they did it, and why it worked. Along the way were a few impostors as well. They were usually exposed in due time by the performance of the company they were heading.

It fascinated me to watch corporations' function. Their leadership, deep-seated values, employee dedication, and quality of the products produced were just a few of the variables I'd seen. Those that ultimately ended up on top also had internal discipline, a necessary ingredient for long-term success, and they knew how to effectively use it.

When the rubber hits the road, when various challenges are hitting you from multiple angles, the ability to keep things balanced is often what separates success from failure. I observed balance in thriving large multinational companies and learned from it.

For me, keeping balanced with a family and a business while remaining focused on my journey had always been a critical and constant challenge when I wore many hats and was being pulled in many personal and professional directions. If one is not careful, it can take a toll on your health. At times I suspect it threatened mine.

Whether on top of a mountain hanging by my fingertips on a cliff face or crossing the finish line of a marathon ten years in a row (having begun running at an age when I could have been sitting at home drawing Social Security), I've encountered a number of unusual but welcome challenges. Meeting them boosted my confidence and changed my attitude. Nothing was impossible if I worked at it, no matter the obstacles.

I've always looked forward to the challenges some might shy away from. It's part of the feeling of being an independent producer, thinking for yourself, making your own decisions, and being recognized for the accomplishment. It can't be manufactured; it has to come from inside.

My passion remains fierce and hasn't changed. What has changed is my complete confidence in knowing how to do it and do it to the fullest.

When I began my odyssey, questions filled my mind. As time passed, those questions were replaced with answers. I developed the acumen to know which questions were real and which ones were empty distractions for a busy mind.

Despite rough waters, I am exactly where I'm supposed to be, careening toward the future. Challenges continue to keep my skin tingling and heart pounding.

A shiver goes down my spine and my stomach fills with anticipation knowing new doors are about to open when I *run the music* on whatever comes next.

ACKNOWLEGEMENTS:

Planning and writing a book can often be a solitary venture. In truth, it takes a team effort for a book to become a reality. There were many who offered encouragement, suggestions, and challenges as my stories began to take shape on the page.

My talented editor Mike Robinson, the author of many books, constantly pushed me to redefine the story, expand its impact, insert the emotion, build the tension and keep writing.

Jennifer Givner, acapellbookcoverdesign@gmail.com, once again stepped up creatively to design a sparkling cover, and meticulously format the book for maximum reader enjoyment. She also designed and formatted my first book, Reaching for Fireflies.

Pat Gainor, patgainor@gmail.com, my beautiful gifted wife, and outstanding artist, provided the background painting on the cover from her large collection of paintings. Her enthusiasm and encouragement meant so much to me during the writing.

I want to express my gratitude to the wonderful writers in the critique group, "Write Night." I had the opportunity to read segments of the book to them each week as it took shape. Their positive attitudes and advice kept me going. The group included a remarkable lineup of accomplished authors and writers: Steven Bourne, Christine Dubois, Leslie Hall, Joe Rice, Neda Gallagher, Liach Grimminger, Cody Carver, Tom Skarshaug, Kai Fu, Jenny Zenner, Pat Schwab.

Also, thanks to the team at Book Baby for their excellent printing and support with the launch.

ABOUT THE AUTHOR:

Following three years serving in the U.S. armed forces, Ed Tar returned home to begin his writing career as a journalist and anchor in radio and television news in Michigan and Ohio. Moving to Los Angeles in the late 1970's, he continued as a writer, and independent producer of television documentaries, short films and live corporate events. His work has been honored with numerous awards from organizations across the U.S. including the International Film and TV Festival of New York, the U. S. Industrial Film Festival, the California Newspaper Ad Executives Association, and the Hollywood Angels Award honoring him for his stirring TV documentary, *Kids, Dreams and Courage.* His work has been featured in several magazines.

He earned his BA degree at the University of Detroit. He currently lives in Los Angeles with his wife, painter and former actress Pat Gainor.

Run The Music is his second book.

His debut memoir: *Reaching For Fireflies* is his powerful story of growing up in Detroit, and the gutsy decision he made, against all odds, to escape the negative, disruptive environment surrounding him at home and find a better path in life.

CONNECT WITH ED TAR:

Website: www.EdTarAuthor.com

Facebook: http://www.facebook.com/ed.tar7

LinkedIn in: http://www.linkedin.com/in/ed-tar-b4407b-4a

Instagram: http://www.instagram.com/edtarassociates

Email: etieta@aol.com